THE
GREAT
SEPARATION

THE
GREAT
SEPARATION

The story of the Boston Tea Party
and the beginning of
the American Revolution

Donald Barr Chidsey

WILDSIDE PRESS

By the Same Author

NOVELS

The Wickedest Pilgrim
Reluctant Cavalier
His Majesty's Highwayman
This Bright Sword
Captain Bashful
Lord of the Isles
Captain Adam
Stronghold
Panama Passage
Nobody Heard the Shot
Each One Was Alone
Weeping Is for Women
Pistols in the Morning

BIOGRAPHY

Elizabeth I
John the Great:
  The Times and Life of John L. Sullivan
The Gentleman from New York:
  A Biography of Roscoe Conkling
Sir Humphrey Gilbert
Sir Walter Raleigh
Marlborough:
  The Portrait of a Conqueror
Bonnie Prince Charlie

JUVENILE
Rod Rides High

Contents

THE
GREAT
SEPARATION

1

SALT WATER TEA

THE YOUNG QUAKER was franky afraid. A bit out of
breath after his return from the Governor's country home
at Milton, he was, at twenty-three, prematurely overweight;
and his eyes popped. Through his family he owned the
greater part of *Dartmouth*, the first and nearest of the three
vessels that rested off Griffin's Wharf.

Tonight was the night that counted, December 16, 1773.
The twenty days allowed for clearance would be ended to-
morrow, and if the tea in *Dartmouth*'s hold had not otherwise been disposed of it could be landed, stored, and sold at
public auction. Bluster, delaying tactics, threats, hereafter
would not avail. Spread-eagle oratory would count for nothing. This was the night.

The young Quaker in truth quaked. He had never before seen so many persons in one place, and all of them glar-
ing at him, all who could get close enough. There must have
been seven thousand men in and immediately outside of the
Old South meeting house that night, men not only from
Boston but from towns as far as twenty miles away. They

were wild-eyed, slavering. Among them, surely, were many
of the dreaded Liberty Boys, shoulder-hitters who roamed
the streets looking for trouble, and who on more than one
night had pulled to pieces the house of some government
official they did not like. They looked, right now, as if they
would welcome a chance to pull almost anything—or anybody—apart. They had nothing against *him*, the young
Quaker—his name was Francis Rotch—and he knew this,
and kept telling it to himself. He was innocent enough, a
mere straw tossed in this blast. All the same, it made him uneasy to stand there in the middle of them and report.

No, he said, the Governor had not consented to give him
a pass for his vessels—in addition to *Dartmouth* the Rotches
owned much of *Beaver*, which also carried East India Company tea—and he could not possibly instruct the skippers to
sail out of the bay and back to England: the guns of Fort
William, for so long shotted, most assuredly would open
up on them. That was the final word. That was what the
Governor had said.

There was a widespread growl, but it was not directed at
Rotch, who indeed after this was ignored.

The crowd had known what he would report, but there
was that growl all the same. The meeting was about to break
up. God knew what would happen next.

A man with steel-gray eyes, a graying, thin-haired,
middle-aged man, waved his arms from the chairman's seat.
He did not look as if he had the will to swat a fly, yet he
was the so-called Master of the Town Meeting, the Whig
political manipulator par excellence, a lifelong member of
the powerful Calkers' or Caucus Club,[1] who could with a
whistle summon to his side uncounted numbers of North End
ruffians. Somehow, weakly flapping his arms, he quieted the
crowd.

"This meeting can do nothing more to save the country," he quavered.

It was a signal. Instantly from the street outside came a succession of ear-splitting yells that were meant to sound like the warwhoops of red men—and that in sober truth were terrifying.

The assemblage surged toward the doors, but the chairman stopped them with a plea for formal adjournment: things should be done right.

"Boston Harbor a teapot tonight," somebody upstairs shouted. "Hurrah for Griffin's Wharf!"

There was some scattered cheering at this, but for the most part the men were orderly, and they let Sam Adams have his proper adjournment.

After that they hurried outside.

It had been raining all day, a Thursday, but now, at nightfall, the sky was clear and the moon was out, lighting a strange scene.

The "Indians" might have numbered twenty, but more were coming all the time. They did little dance steps, waggling the axes or hatchets they held in the manner of flaunted tomahawks. They grunted "Ugh" and "How" to each other, and sometimes, "Me know you," a salutation obviously agreed upon in advance. Some were elaborately costumed, but most wore slap-dash outfits no doubt improvised in haste: blankets or parts of blankets wrapped around their middles, a few feathers thrust into their caps or their hair, and some form of face coloring, not necessarily red, often enough a simple stovepipe soot.

They kept appearing, from all directions.

The whoops and the dancing soon ceased. These were not celebrants but serious men on a serious mission. When enough of them had assembled they paired off, and at the command of their gaily bedight "chiefs" they marched, two by two, down Milk Street, spectators tumbling on either side. They turned into Hutchinson Street,² past Fort Hill on the way to the waterfront. There might have been seventy or eighty of them by that time; but the procession was a quiet one, almost sedate.

Boston was wide-awake. Candles were being lighted everywhere, and people were calling questions from windows.

Apprentices, young men, a few not more than boys, with or without some semblance of aboriginal garb, were attaching themselves to the party, eager to help, perky, birdlike in their movements.

Griffin's Wharf, opposite the place where Hutchinson Street emptied into Flounder Lane, was a roofed structure. Tonight it was guarded; but this was not a guard likely to hold off the braves, for it had been mounted, day and night for the past three weeks, by the Sons of Liberty themselves, its purpose being to make sure that nobody removed the tea from those three vessels. So far from blocking them, indeed, the guards fell open before the "Indians," who broke up smartly into three squads, each with its own captain and bosun, each assigned to a separate vessel.

Dartmouth, Eleanor, Beaver, two ships and a brig, were tied up in that order, *Dartmouth* being athwart the wharf, so that all that was needed to go from one to another was an easy climb over a couple of side-by-side gunnels. Anchors were down, but they were not at that time acting in restraint, for the tide was so low that the heavily laden vessels actually rested on the bottom.

Perhaps by prearrangement all captains were absent, but the mates were summoned topside and told that nobody would be hurt and nothing would be touched but the tea itself and the slings and cranes needed to hoist it out of the holds. There was no hilarity, no confusion. Each had his assigned task. There was no resistance.

The clunk of hatchets was loud in the air, but otherwise everything was quiet. Thousands, fascinated, watched. Nobody even dreamed of interfering.

The thin wooden lids gave little trouble, but each chest was additionally sheathed in a heavy burlap sack which proved to be unexpectedly tough. Once it was axed open, each case was carried to a rail and its contents and later the empty container itself were dumped overside. Boys light enough to wallow in the mud beneath the wharf from there poked at it with barrel staves, pushing it out into the Bay, across which a faint breeze carried it in long iridescent windrows toward Dorchester.

There were three hundred and forty-two chests in all, and every one of them was emptied. Though this was mid-December, plenty of sweat poured. "I never worked so hard in my life before," one "Indian" said afterward.

They started a little before nine o'clock. They finished a little before midnight. They were scrupulously careful about the vessels themselves and the hoisting apparatus. The only thing that was damaged was a padlock, the personal property of one of the skippers; and for this they apologized.

They swept up afterward.

They got together on the dock for a counting of noses, and there each man took off his boots or shoes and shook them out. The debris was swept overboard.[3]

They left in the same semimilitary manner in which they had come, two by two, keeping step, their hatchets shouldered. They broke up quietly, a few at a time, going their several ways; and by one o'clock there was not a soul in sight.

The next morning somebody who did not linger, and did not leave his name, replaced the damaged padlock with a new one.

CHAPTER

2

THE SUGAR SNOBS

W<small>HY?</small>
What caused reputable men to stay up so late at night
deliberately destroying some £18,000 worth of private property? They must have known that they were sowing a whirl-
wind, if not, as the event proved, a war. Why, then, did they
do it?

The saying that England conquered half of the world in
a fit of absent-mindedness is droll but false. The thing was
carefully planned. When the Seven Years' War [4] ended, in
1763, what John Strachey has called the most successfully
greedy nation in history looked around to gloat over spoils
that were without precedent, including as they did virtually
all of India, much of North America, and a sizable smattering
of West Indian islands, besides, pointedly, undisputed command of the seven seas.

Even before the Treaty of Paris, the loot was being
carefully counted. As early as 1761 the men at Whitehall
were debating whether when France was beaten to her knees

Guadeloupe or Canada should be taken from her; and there were those, the great Pitt among them, who favored taking *both* and who were to think for the rest of their lives that England had been over-generous.

At first glance it might seem a curious choice to arise, but the West Indies, the sugar islands, were very highly esteemed in those days, whereas Canada, though it did produce a beaver pelt now and then, was for the most part a vast frozen wasteland. Adam Smith was working on, but had not yet published, his *Wealth of Nations*, and mercantilism still was in the saddle. Mercantilism meant the establishment of a system under which you sold to your neighbors more than you bought from them, and thereby made money. What happened when your neighbors ran short of cash or payments in kind was not asked. Mercantilism presupposed huge size, and the gigantic new British Empire seemed to have been developed for this very purpose. No, there was not any absent-mindedness connected with it. The men at Whitehall acted with all convenient calculation.

Political rather than economic considerations, however, might have dictated the ultimate choice of Canada. The mainland colonies of America were not thought much of in England, though trade with them increased every year. The southern colonies produced indigo, rice, and naval stores for the mother country (the pre-Eli Whitney cotton crop there was negligible) and this was good, if unexciting. The middle and northern colonies produced some foodstuffs, which were acceptable, and ships and naval supplies, which were most welcome. From time to time these latter colonies might make a feeble attempt to establish industries of their own, but such attempts customarily were nipped in the bud by a London alerted by representatives of those same industries at Home. Thus, when it was proposed to build some small slitting mills and rolling mills in Pennsylvania and New York the English steelmakers were quick to squawk, and Parliament spoke up, saying "No"; and when in 1731 American-made beaver hats began to appear in English shops the honorable Company of Feltmakers promptly petitioned Parliament to put a stop to this trade and to limit all American hat makers to two apprentices, and once again Parliament obliged, going even further by prohibiting any intercolonial trade in hats. On the other hand, when the British shipbuilders complained that American shipbuilders were outselling them and asked for relief, Parliament emphatically refused. England always needed ships, and needed them now more desperately than ever, but her own forests were almost depleted, whereas there was still plenty of standing timber at or near all of the American seacoasts. It was not feared, in England, that America ever would amount to much industrially, for the reason that labor was so high there, but the case of the shipyards constituted a happy exception. If England did not get that timber and gear from the American colonies she would have to get it from Scandinavia or Russia at a greater cost, for her own home supplies were not enough. So—the trade should be kept within the limits of the Empire, whenever this was possible. Mercantilism again.[5] The colonies existed to feed the mother country materials—preferably raw materials—that the mother country could not conveniently get for herself on the open world market; and the colonies, of course, should buy all of their manufactured products from Home. There was nothing uniquely English about this system, which was practiced everywhere. England indeed had been lax in dealing with her American mainland colonies, which is what caused the trouble when at the end of the Seven Years' War she announced her intention of pulling the strings tighter. The continental colonies had been, bluntly, spoiled. They demanded too much, took too much for granted. France, Denmark, Holland, Portugal, and Spain were much stricter with *their* settlements. There were those who thought that so far the New World children had brought themselves up reasonably well, all things considered. Burke spoke of the "salutary neglect" with which they had been treated. But all that must end now. The colonies must be driven back into line. They were growing up. They must learn how to obey.

It could well be that the Sugar Aristocracy had something to do with England's choice of Canada rather than Guadeloupe. They were a highly articulate lot, those ex-islanders. The mainland colonists depended upon agents stationed in London to represent their respective interests, men who might or might not be members of Parliament but who in any event were widely acquainted in Parliamentary circles and presumably assiduous in looking after the welfare of their employers so far away. The members of the Sugar Aristocracy plunged right in, playing the Parliamentary game as they found it—and they found it very dirty.[6]

The islands planter had an advantage over the mainland planter in that after a little while he did not have to do any work. He simply appointed a manager—who was often a lawyer, often too a cheat—and went home to live on the profits. They were fond of display, these men and their ladies, given to giddy carriages, brave clothes. They liked to dazzle. But they could spend money on other things as well, and since their whole life was conditioned by the price of sugar—for the islands were a one-crop group—it behooved them, or they thought that it behooved them, to see that the mercantile system was kept going at top speed and in their favor. The best way to do this was by being in Parliament, right there. Seats did not have to be earned. They could be bought over the counter, just like any other commodity. And buy them the Sugar Aristocracy did.

There were five native-born mainland Americans serving in the House of Commons, all through by-elections, in the years 1768–1783, though there were a few others who had visited America and others still who sometimes traded there. All of these were, presently, full-time Englishmen. They seldom acted together and had little weight.

There were only thirteen native West Indians in the Commons during this same period, but there were many others who were landowners in the islands, having inherited their holdings, which in most cases they had not even taken the trouble to visit. They were much more powerful than the simple figures would seem to show, however, for through family connections and the out-and-out purchase of votes the Sugar Aristocracy was credited with an average bag of about forty members.

Such personages could hardly be expected to take anything but a dim view of the proposal to annex the sugar-rich, competing island of Guadeloupe to the Empire. Neither did they approve of the lax way in which the mainland Colonies were treated.

The mainland colonies were divided into three groups: the southern colonies from Maryland to Georgia inclusive (East and West Florida, additional loot from the Seven Years' War, were in British hands but had almost no communication with the other colonies); the middle colonies of Pennsylvania, Delaware, New Jersey, and New York; and the New England colonies, Connecticut, Massachusetts, Rhode Island, and New Hampshire (Vermont was a disputed territory, Maine still a part of Massachusetts). The southern states were agricultural, their planters at the mercy of British merchants and thus, habitually, increasingly, in debt. The middle and New England states had developed a not inconsiderable trade with the mother country, but this trade was largely one-way. For instance, Franklin told the House of Commons that his employer, Pennsylvania, bought £500,000 worth of goods a year in England and sent back raw materials valued at £40,000. Much the same thing could be said for each of the other middle and northern colonies. English merchants necessarily extended long-term and (for the period) low-interest credits to their American customers; but even so, this could not go on; for sooner or later the colonies would run out of money, and every move they made to print their own was balked by a watchful Board of Trade and Plantations. Some other market must be found in order that the upper colonists should not go deeper and deeper into debt, as the poor southerners were doing. This was found in the sugar islands.

A West Indian planter, or the manager of a plantation absentee-owned, might have a small kitchen garden for his own table—known locally as "ground provisions"—or he might send out a houseboy to fish for him; but that would not take care of the slaves, the field hands, for whom great quantities of cheap food were needed, since the islands, any island down there, produced little but sugar cane. This is where the Yankee trader appeared. He sent barrel staves and horses, always in demand in those parts, down to such English colonies as Jamaica and Barbados, but most of all he sent dried fish, salted beef, and ship's biscuit. He was paid, generally, with molasses.

There were two kinds of molasses.[7] The heavy dark thick by-product of the crushing mill, right on the plantation, was molasses to Americans and British alike. The partly refined cane—"clayed sugar" it was called—was then packed into barrels (made of New England staves and hoops, like as not) and sent to England, where a second, lighter syrup was given off in the final refining process. This was called "treacle," though to Americans it was all molasses. It was the heavy, earlier product that was such an American trade staple in the eighteenth century.[8]

Molasses could be used for sweetening bread or it could be poured over flapjacks, but very little of it was. Most of it went into making rum. The English, who were not notably fond of rum, shied away from buying large amounts of molasses. The Americans had no choice; and so, loaded, they perforce distilled rum. New England alone was turning out 1,260,000 gallons of rum a year when the troubles with the mother country started.[9]

It wasn't very good rum. Most of it was the variety known as Kill-Devil, fit only for chiefs of the African slave coast, where it was the accepted currency, and for Indians, who would drink anything, though immense quantities were consumed by white men as well.

The molasses did not need to be British molasses, though it was *supposed* to be that. It was possible, at a place like, say, Kingston, to purchase barrels duly branded as of that colony and as containing molasses, though in fact they were empty. With these, and at a slight additional fee, you could get a formal clearance testifying that this was indeed your cargo. You then went to nearby St. Eustatius or St. Croix or Martinique and had the barrels filled with Dutch or Danish or French molasses, which was so much cheaper. Holland and Denmark, being small nations, did not need much molasses. France, at the demand of the cognac interests, who feared that rum would cut into their profits, forbade it—another example of mercantilism—and the French colonies thus would sell the stuff for almost nothing.

The Sugar Aristocracy did not look with favor on this practice.

Enterprising New Englanders had soon developed this molasses-based traffic into a three-way route. They took the rum to Africa, where they bought slaves with it. They took the slaves to the West Indies, where they sold them, being paid in molasses. They took the molasses back to New England, where it was made into rum, most of which was sent to Africa to buy slaves, which were taken to the West Indies. . . . Some of the most respectable family fortunes in those parts had this triangular trade as their foundation.

The so-called Navigation Acts of the seventeenth century were designed to regulate trade rather than to raise a revenue. They were not harsh, not arbitrary, and were not resented in the mainland colonies, where indeed only one of them, the supplementary Molasses Act of 1733—it was to run only four years but it was renewed again and again—was disliked. Even this was only a nuisance.

The Molasses Act put a tariff of six pence a gallon on molasses imported from foreign colonies. This was preposterous. It was as much as the molasses itself was worth. Enforced, it would have ruined most of the mainland colonies within a year.

The colonists met this threat by simply ignoring the Molasses Act. True, there were certain formalities that had to be gone through with. The commonest thing was to run most of your cargo ashore in one of the little creeks or bays in Long Island Sound or Narragansett Bay or almost any other convenient inlet—and the coast was studded with such: it might have been specifically designed for smuggling—and then go into a legitimate port and declare and pay for the balance. Everybody would co-operate, for smuggling was a way of life, an accepted practice to which no shame was attached. If by any chance you *were* caught, what jury would convict you? None.

An even simpler way to evade the Molasses Act—unless you wished to get a false clearance in the islands, as already described—was to sail right into a port of entry and pay the customs officer to look the other way while you unloaded. He was not the original appointee to the post. *That* personage would still be in London, where it was possible that he might snag another sinecure. He would be drawing three-quarters of the pay, and contemptuously tossing the other quarter to his deputy, who was doing the real work three thousand miles away. The deputy could not live on so little; nor was he expected to. He could and undoubtedly would turn his head whenever asked.

After the Treaty of Paris, however, Whitehall laid out, and saw through the two houses of Parliament, a whole series of much stricter navigation acts, the most notable of which was the Sugar Act of 1764. This Sugar Act cut the tariff on foreign molasses from six pence to three pence, but—it was to be enforced.

The Home government was firm about this. Heavy penalties were provided for. The sundry customs inspectors who were lolling in London coffee houses were told to get busy or get out. What's more, they were thereafter to live on their salaries. The Navy was alerted, and every naval officer was made a special customs agent, to proceed pretty much as he pleased, whether on the high seas or off soundings or even ashore. Small fast vessels were provided, vessels that could be used to chase smugglers far up streams and shallow bays. Writs of assistance, by means of which customs collectors could break in almost anywhere at any time, provided it was daylight, were authorized; and in the event of a mistake the injured citizen could not sue the government. Most startling of all, persons suspected of violating this Sugar Act of 1764 would not be tried in a provincial criminal court, as previously, but in an admiralty court—and in the admiralty courts there were no juries.

Smuggling, the Home government said, simply *must* be stopped.

CHAPTER

3

THE LUCKY CARD PLAYER

IT WAS A SUDDEN April shower, and Frederick, Prince of Wales, together with his Princess, found themselves stranded and temporarily idle in the royal tent at the races at Egham. Neither being, by any stretch of imagination, an intellectual, a person whose own company was agreeable to himself, they called for a game of whist: they had to do *something*, didn't they? A third hand was quickly found, but it took some time to drum up a fourth, and this, when at last it materialized in the form of James Stuart, Earl of Bute, proved to be a quiet, amiable, adaptable, amenable, and until this time almost shamelessly obscure Scot, who, however, played a good game of whist. Bute's conversation may not have been elevating, but neither the Prince nor the Princess cared much for elevating conversation anyway, and with them, and in particular with the Princess, milord became an instant favorite.

That was in the year 1747, and before the rain was over history had slipped into yet another groove.

A courtier in London then had his choice of two social circles—the King's, which was almost unbelievably dull but in the nature of it the more influential, or that of the Prince of Wales, which if not notably effectual at least wasn't staid.

The King, George II, hated the Prince of Wales, and the Queen too, the remarkable Caroline of Anspach, shared in this detestation of their son. The King and the Prince of Wales had not spoken in years, and Freddy, as he was contemptuously rather than affectionately called, maintained his own establishment at Leicester House. The situation was hardly edifying; but neither was it new, and it did have in its favor the air of being a family tradition, for George II, presently the King, when *he* was Prince of Wales had hated with a hatred as black and bitter as gall *his* father, George I, who reciprocated this feeling.

Thus there were two courts in London, and if you were anybody at all you belonged to one of them (you could not belong to both). Lord Bute until this time had not been anybody at all, his presence, his company not in demand; but after that providential shower at Egham he became, abruptly, a very important personage. His whist game continued to be pleasant and painless, but he developed, most unexpectedly, a talent for backstairs intrigue. Here was a first-class courtier, ambitious, relentless, unobtrusive, and even equipped with a reputation for philandering in high places, for he was widely believed to be the Princess's lover. Sometimes there is truth in royal household scandal, and though there is nothing to indicate that such was the case here, the indubitable fact remains that the rumor flourished. The English have always disliked the occupant of the office of royal favorite, whether male or female, but especially male, and Bute soon became an object of scorn. Cartoonists delighted to picture him in the company of a jackboot—a pun on his title, which is pronounced "boot"—and a petticoat, representing the Princess.

In 1750 Bute was made lord of the bedchamber at Leicester House, where, definitely, he was the man to see; and when Freddy died the following year milord took over the practical political education of Freddy's son, another George, the heir to the throne.

George was a pudgy pop-eyed boy, shy, serious, uncertain of himself. "Be king, Georgie," his mother would say to him, and his preceptor hammered into him early the need to split the all-powerful Whig party so that he could rule in truth when his time came, a policy that was to have its reflection in the misunderstanding on the other side of the sea.[10]

When the third George did ascend to the throne, in 1760, at the age of twenty-two, he had a clear idea not only of what he wanted but of how he ought to go about getting it. Bute, at least at first, strove to stay out of sight; but he was a prodigiously busy man.

The system was simple. The government was to be a reversion to what it had been when young George's great-grandfather, George I, took over—that is, it was to be a real kingship, with the monarch setting policy and distributing patronage in person rather than through ministers. Parties if possible were to be put down; at least they were to be subdued, kept in place. George III meant to be a ruler, not just a symbol. The speeches from the throne would actually *come* from the throne.

This was not to be a tyranny. George III never thought of himself as a despot. He only meant to take what he believed was rightly his—to take back, that is, the privileges and prerogatives that would have belonged to his grandfather and great-grandfather if those two had not been much more interested in their mistresses and in revisits to their beloved Herrenhausen in Germany. George III was not reaching for anything that he was not entitled to, in his own eyes, but he did want everything that he thought he *was* entitled to.

It was much remarked at the time of his accession that he was the first King of England born *in* England for half a century. George I never had troubled to learn the language of a country he clearly abhorred. George II had been hard to understand. Even Freddy, the late departed papa, had had a muddy accent, though he at least did consent to sleep with English women. But here, now, was the real thing. Not too bright perhaps; but a king does not need to be bright. His morals were impeccable—he was a devout family man—and even his manners were not bad.

"I glory in the name of Briton," he announced promptly, and this sent a thrill through the hearts of many. It was only when they had fallen to thinking it over that some of them wondered why he had said "Briton" instead of "Englishman." Would that scheming Scot back there have anything to do with it? The scheming Scot assuredly did.

The King who wished to do away with parties proposed to accomplish this by starting a party of his own, the "King's Men." These were largely recruited for him by Lord Bute, who naturally brought many of his friends down from Scotland. The newcomers, uncouth in the eyes of the English, and all but unintelligible, were to be found everywhere, in all sorts of offices. Men fell to muttering about the "foul northern invasion," and Bute himself not infrequently was referred to as "the Scotch menace," for many Englishmen, especially at just that time, agreed with Samuel Johnson, who in 1763, when mention was made of the noble prospects of Scotland, cried: "But, sir, let me tell you, the noblest prospect which a Scotchman ever sees, is the high road that leads him to England!" Not since the appearance in England of the first Stuart king, James I, who was surrounded and tailed by a ravenous horde of Caledonians, had Scotland been so virulently disliked by its neighbor to the south. What's more, the arrivals, duly trained, insisted upon selling their votes to the King instead of to the Whig leaders, a course which, while not actually illegal, was widely thought unsporting.

OTIS.   GEORGE III.   LORD MANSFIELD.
GRENVILLE.   BUTE.

I. THE ENGLISH LEADERS

In the business of egging the Whigs to fight among themselves Lord Bute was diabolically clever. Granted, he had been given a good start. The Whigs had been swollen by a long period of prosperity and power and they were already snarling and snapping at one another, so that all Bute needed to do was bring the fight out into the open and intensify it; and this he did do supremely well.

It was unfortunate for him that though he was only carrying out the wishes of his monarch he was made to appear personally to blame for the resignation of William Pitt. Pitt, at the height of his genius, was a public hero. It might almost be said that he had won the Seven Years' War single-handed, and it did seem a pity that he was allowed no part in the framing of the peace.

Bute became the most hated man in Great Britain. He was often hissed, several times his carriage was stoned, and he did not dare to show himself in the streets without a bodyguard of pugilists. But he was faithful to his king, whom he served doggedly and well. The Whigs in time were routed.

After Pitt, who was in a class by himself, the Whig to bring down was the most marvelously muddle-headed Duke of Newcastle, the chief favors-peddler of the party, the man who presided over the pie counter. Newcastle had been secretary of state and was presently prime minister, relieving the august Pitt of all routine dirty work. He was very rich and very industrious, though he usually bit off more than he could chew: it was said of him by one who knew him well, Lord Wilmington, that he "always loses half an hour in the morning which he is running after the rest of the day without ever being able to overtake it." It was also said of him that he never had time to read the dispatches from the colonial governors, which accumulated in great piles in his closet; and while this may be something of an exaggeration it is certain that Newcastle did not know much, if he could be said to know anything at all, about America.

The duke had been running Parliamentary politics for so long, and he had such sound connections, and so much money, that he could scarcely believe it when he found himself—for nothing!—chucked out. He was badly bewildered, and never really did recover from the shock.

Bute took the center of the stage for a while, though he persistently averred that there was no such person as a prime minister. But he was a man who preferred to work from behind the scenes, and once Pitt and Newcastle were out and the King's Men were firmly in he persuaded George III to appoint a quite different person to be head of the government, he himself planning to fade into the background.

The new man was George Grenville, who had married into the Temple family, sometimes called "Cobham's Cubs," an institution. He was like Newcastle in that he was industrious; but the comparison stops there. Grenville had a neat mind. A "dry, precise man of great knowledge and industry, almost always right in little matters and very patient of the misapprehension of less exact people," [11] he was all business, a stiff, unpleasant, dour man. Grenville *did* read the dispatches from America, and he was appalled by the picture of inefficiency that they drew. He resolved that this must be straightened out, this mess. He said as much.

Grenville not only steered the Sugar Act through Parliament and tightened all anti-smuggling precautions in the colonies, but he also announced that he would soon introduce a Stamp Act. That was his undoing.

CHAPTER

4

MR. GRENVILLE LAYS

IT ON THE LINE

THE ART OF TAXATION consists in so plucking the goose as to obtain the largest amount of feathers with the least possible amount of hissing." This definition has been attributed to the great French financier-statesman, Jean Baptiste Colbert, who flourished in the middle of the seventeenth century. It may be that Grenville never heard it. He would have disapproved if he did. Not only was it irreverent: it was inaccurate. Taxation to him was a mental exercise, a much more intricate business than the mere vulgar plucking of a goose.

He was not rash! He perfectly realized that his motives might be misunderstood—so many persons being slow of comprehension, as was made evident by the flood of protests against the Sugar Act, protests that went unheeded and conceivably even unread; and he proceeded with care. Polysyllabic, polite, infinitely patient, he pronounced his words, as it were, with a full mouth, with the elaborate slowness of one who explains something obvious to a half-wit.

He had prepared the ground. He had sent out scouts,

made inquiries of colonial governors, studied reports, piled up figures. Mr. Grenville had great faith in figures.

He called in the agents of the various colonies, the men who represented them in London. He explained the situation.

A stamp act clearly was the fairest and simplest means of taxation. It was not new; it had been tried in Great Britain, and found effective. It was no trouble. It provided that stamped paper be used on official documents—deeds, leases, contracts, court orders, marriage licenses, etc.—and that was all. He had given ample warning of his intention, a whole year of warning, when he introduced the Sugar Act, saying at that time that a stamp act probably would be needed as a supplement. Meanwhile, if the individual colonies could think of any better way of paying a part of their financial share in the Empire, why, Mr. Grenville was willing to listen to them. Was that clear?

The agents, to a man, opined that their colonies would not look with favor upon a tax that was imposed from the outside and was for revenue purposes only. They would prefer, the agents said, the old system of royal requisitions.

Grenville waved this aside. Requisitions, demonstratively, were inefficient. Look at what had happened in the course of the late war, when Great Britain, her back to the wall, had asked the colonies, through her gracious King, for some financial help. Men the colonies would supply—fighters, yes— but they expected them to be paid by the Crown. And as for money requisitions, when these were raised at all it was only after long and bitter argument. They never could be counted upon. No, requisitions were a thing of the past, a holdover from medieval times. But if the colonies had some other plan, some system of their own to suggest—

The agents said that they would ask. But, how would each colony know how much was expected of it, and also how much its neighbors would be expected to raise?

They could confer on that, Grenville replied. They could compare notes.

Here he was palpably wrong. The colonies had no machinery for conference. As Grenville had every reason to know, they were a hodgepodge, a mishmash of different religions and different nationalities, and their forms of government too differed. A New Yorker hated a New Englander more than he did a Frenchman; a backcountry Carolinian hated a planter from the coast; and so it went. Each colony had a governor, but two, Connecticut and Rhode Island, had such liberal charters that for purposes of local government they were independent states; and these elected their own governors. Each colony had an elected house of representatives and a council, and the council in most cases, but not in all, was a sort of upper legislative house and was appointed by the governor. They had no common capital, no headquarters; they yielded no standard product or crop; even the climates were wide-ranging. The boundaries were erratic, seldom natural, and not always well established. Two of the colonies, Pennsylvania and Maryland, were proprietorial—that is, owned by families, respectively Penn and Calvert—which made for further confusion. Only in Virginia and Maryland was the Church of England officially established, while in New England, the congregationalists ruled the roost, and in Pennsylvania, the Quakers, though outnumbered, held all the political power in their hands.

How could such colonies get together in a common place and agree upon anything at all, much less upon anything so complicated and touchy as to how much taxes to pay and in what form to pay them? It was absurd, as Grenville should have known.

Moreover, the home government distinctly did not *wish* the colonies to get together. Separate and squabbling, they were weak. United, howsoever loosely, they might prove strong. For they were growing. The mainlanders, with presently a population of 1,775,000—as compared with 8,500,000 for Great Britain—were increasing like guinea pigs. They were *doubling* their population every thirty years, and it was estimated that they would overtake the population of Britain by 1810,[12] and what would happen then, if they were working in harness?

The only place that was equipped to suggest what the colonies should pay was London itself, Whitehall. Undoubtedly Grenville knew this, but he preferred to make no mention of it. It would dim somewhat the glow he felt when he contemplated his own liberality.

Grenville was on firmer ground when he set forth his statistics. Statistics, he knew, never lied.

Great Britain had come out of the war master of a good part of the habitable globe; but the cost had been staggering. The national debt was now £158,000,000, more, much more, than anybody or any nation had ever owed before. The interest on it was £5,000,000 a year, a crushing load. It was not proposed that the colonies be taxed in order to pay some of this back, reduce the debt. It was proposed only to tax the colonies in order to help pay part of *their own expenses*, that was all. Before the war, Grenville pointed out, the American civil and military establishments had cost the home country £70,000 a year. The figure now stood at £350,000 a year, and was going up.

The Stamp Act had been framed to raise about £60,000 a year, which would average out at one shilling a head, certainly not excessive, gentlemen? The public debt of all the American colonies put together amounted to just about eighteen shillings a head; but that of Great Britain amounted to eighteen *pounds*, twenty times as much.

The average Englishman paid twenty-five shillings a year

in taxes of all sorts. The average American paid six pence, or one-fiftieth as much.

The Sugar Act was not in itself the answer. Until that had been passed and until it was rigidly enforced, Grenville told them, it was costing the home government £8,ooo to collect every £2,ooo in customs duties. Was that, gentlemen, good business?

Benjamin Franklin, called before the House of Commons, asserted that the colonies—or at least the houses of representatives of those colonies, the larger and more noisy part of each legislature—would consent to any *external* tax, such as a trade regulation, or a customs duty, but they might well object to any *internal* tax, a heading under which the Stamp Act surely would come, on the ground that only they, the legislatures, had a right to lay a tax upon themselves.

Americans were entitled to their constitutional rights as Englishmen even though they did not happen to be living in England, the agents pointed out, and one constitutional right of an Englishman is to refuse to pay a tax that he has not consented to.

Grenville thought that this discrimination between internal and external taxes was absurd. A tax was a tax, he said; or, as a member of Parliament was to put it, soon afterward: "What a pother, whether the money is to be taken out of their coat-pocket or out of their waistcoat-pocket!"

So that was that, finished Grenville, in effect, and what would the colonies do about it?

He soon got his answer.

CHAPTER

5

THE HILLBILLY

IT HAD BEEN SUPPOSED that if there was any trouble it would start in Boston. Massachusetts was the hotbed of dissatisfaction, and Boston was the hotbed of Massachusetts. A town of about 15,000, it fairly sputtered, like a lighted bomb.

Englishmen, puzzled at the colonists' insistence upon representation in Parliament if they were to be taxed by that body, pointed out that the colonies were in truth represented in the Commons by some of the finest orators. Look at Burke, they cried. Look at Pitt. And there were others. To this the colonists would reply that they wanted their own men or none; they did not want volunteers from the outside, men who might be replaced by other-minded members when they came to die or to retire, or who might themselves change their stand and cease their championship of a part of the world that had begun to vex them.

One of the most spectacular of these champions was Lieutenant Colonel Isaac Barré, a French Huguenot from Ireland, who had fought in America under Wolfe, and who fought quite as ferociously now in the Commons against taxation of the American colonies. The colonel did not believe in half-way measures, and he was eloquent and could be a fearsome sight when he shook his fists as he raged, the long dark ugly bullet wound on his left cheek throbbing.

It was Barré who had given the Americans one of their happiest phrases. Angered by a speaker who had referred to the coddling of the colonists and had demanded to know how much more interest in them Parliament had to take before they would subside, Barré sprang to his feet with a hot retort: "As soon as you began to care about them, that care was exercised in sending persons to rule them in one department and another, who were, perhaps, the deputies of deputies to some members of this house, sent to spy out their liberties, to misrepresent their actions, and to prey upon them; men whose behavior on many occasions has caused the blood of these sons of liberty to recoil within them."

He had spoken extemporaneously, but the "sons of liberty" phrase was gleefully picked up across the sea, where the colonists were grateful.[18] Sons of Liberty sprang up in all the cities, and these were to prove useful, though sometimes, through over-exuberance, dangerous. Like the volunteer firemen of a later generation, the Sons of Liberty tended to be an unstable amalgam of patriotism, sociability, and political activity, with now and then a dash of rowdyism.

The Sons of Liberty did not originate in Boston, but they did flourish there, and early, among the first. Mobbery was one of the ways in which the age expressed itself, but much of it was pointless, a mere blowing off of steam at someone else's expense. The Sons of Liberty gave the mobs some cohesion and even a shadow of an excuse. In Boston the movement resulted in a bringing-together of the two worst gangs, the North Enders and the South Enders, who until this time had fought whenever they happened to meet and whose November

5 brawl was an annual classic. Instead of marching around
singing "Remember, remember/ The fifth of November/ The
Gunpowder treason and plot!" as young street toughs did
elsewhere in the Empire and of course in England on that
holiday, dragging with them an effigy of Guy Fawkes [14]
which in time would be tossed upon a bonfire, the North
Enders and the South Enders of Boston constructed rude
"Popes." Then they strode to the center of the city and each
side tried to capture the other side's Pope. More than the
effigies, then, were battered and banged. The battles, indeed,
got more fierce every year—until the Sons of Liberty brought
the two sides together.

Boston for years had been one of the principal smuggling
ports. Fortunes had been made there in illegal trade—fortunes
such as that of the late Thomas Hancock, who, being childless,
left all his money to his nephew John, sometimes called King
John because of the pretentiousness of his establishment, a
slim, short, dandified, insufferably vain man who, despite his
vast commercial and real estate interests, was a convinced
Whig.

It was in Boston that there lived and often raved that
brilliant, unpredictable lawyer, James Otis, whose words were
made of fire, who could turn a once sedate town meeting into
a yammering rabble, and in Boston too that Otis's pyrotechnics
were backed stolidly and solidly, steadily too, by the frail,
persistent Samuel Adams, a man who never ceased to struggle.

It was in Boston that the *Gazette*—Tories called it "the
weekly dung barge"—plumped again and again for utter independence, a word most Americans at that time did not even
dare to speak aloud.

Boston had its Liberty Tree; it had its Common, where
militiamen determinedly drilled; it had its Beacon Hill, near
the top of which, if rumors were true, a barrel of tar was at all

times hidden, in readiness for the sending-forth of an alarm; it had its patriot horsemen, booted and spurred, ready to ride forth and spread enspiriting news. Boston, in all truth, was the logical location for the first flare-up, if flare-up there was to be.

Massachusetts, of which Boston was the capital, was ruled, in a manner of speaking, by a career administrator named Francis Bernard, a man who aspired to and eventually was to get a baronetcy—but not while he was still in America. He was an earnest, eager official, who had ideas of his own as to how the colony should be governed, but who was kept from putting these ideas into effect by a General Court (the Massachusetts legislature) the lower house of which was largely controlled by the so-called "Boston seat" of four indefatigible Whigs, while the council was not appointed by the governor, as in the other colonies (Connecticut and Rhode Island always excepted) but popularly elected. Bernard tried hard, but he was a man with a living to make, as the Whigs well knew. He was not paid by the Crown but by the colony of Massachusetts Bay, and the General Court held the purse strings.[15] The legislators, however, could not see his reports to the men at Whitehall, and in these he spread himself. Bernard thought that the rest of the Massachusetts Bay colony would fall back into line if only Boston could be humbled. He said so, often.

Second in command was that rarity in Government House, a native son. Thomas Hutchinson not only had been born in Massachusetts but he came from a five-generation colonial family: he was a great-great-grandson of that Anne Hutchinson who had been booted out of Boston early in the seventeenth century because of her advanced theological thought. He had had a career almost automatically distinguished, having been a representative, a councillor, judge of probate, and chief justice, besides lieutenant governor. He was still the last three, all at once, besides being in his capacity of lieutenant governor an ex officio member of the council. A Harvard graduate, and well off, he was engaged in writing a monumental history of the colony in which he had always lived. Hutchinson was altogether admirable, but he was not lovable. He made the wrong enemies. He was intensely patriotic, though not as patriotism would have been defined by the wily, virtually indestructible Sam Adams, "that Son of Sedition, that Master of the Puppets," as Hutchinson called him. Hutchinson too was of the opinion that a few hotheads in Boston were causing all the trouble and that if they were put back into their proper places all would be well again; and he too said this, in letter after letter, report after report, for he was not a man of reserve.[16]

The ways of politics are strange. It was not Massachusetts from which the first loud note of dissent came, after all, but Virginia—Virginia of the fox-hunting, hard-drinking squires, the tiny towns, the utter absence of industry, the foreign merchants, the Church of England, and Patrick Henry.

There had been protests before this, but polite, well-mannered protests, papers filled with insistence that the colonies were loyal to the King, God bless him. These might have been read informally, off the record; but they were not read in Parliament, which refused to receive them.[17] Though the colonies had been given a year in which to think it over, and told that any different ideas they might have would be heeded, when they objected their objections were not even read aloud. General Henry Seymour Conway,[18] another of the outspoken and eloquent friends of the colonies in the House of Commons, made this point in the debate—if it could be called a debate—of February 6, 1765. The House was not interested.

There was amazingly little opposition to the Stamp Act when it came up on first reading, February 13, and it was

"... how the man could speechify!"

2. PATRICK HENRY

passed easily. It was passed on second reading, two days later, without even a division. March 22 it was made into law. It was to go into effect November 1.

At first there was not much more interest in the Stamp Act in the colonies themselves, where the thing just did not seem possible. Some, like Francis Bernard and Thomas Hutchinson, had been against the measure, and had said so in their dispatches, but believed that as long as it was law it should be obeyed. Others, like Daniel Dulaney of Maryland and John Dickinson of Pennsylvania, learnèd lawyers both, took up their pens and made fine pamphlets in opposition to the Stamp Act, but though these were widely read and warmly praised they did nothing to change the fact that the act would really go into effect come November 1. There were a few flaming speeches, but not as many as might have been expected. Even in incandescent Boston, where Oxenbridge Thacher, James Otis, and Samuel Adams labored mightily to raise a wind, there was little response—until Patrick Henry blew off, down south.

He was a wild-eyed man from the Virginia hills, fixedly uncouth, inexorably homespun. At the age of twenty-four, having first failed at sundry other lines, he was admitted to the bar after only six weeks of reading Coke upon Littleton and the Virginia statutes; and already he had plenty of business. He was widely read in history and in the classics—the latter, however, he did not dare to quote back in his home country. He talked like the hillbilly he was, but how the man could speechify!

He had been only nine days in the House of Burgesses when, on May 29, he rose to offer a set of resolves that was to make him famous. Ordinarily he would not have made much of an impression in the Burgesses, for the tidewater planters who controlled that body were smooth, bland, sophisticated men who would have no truck with histrionics, and looked upon the hill people as barbarians; but Henry had picked his time well, or else he was lucky.

It was a sizzling hot day, late in the afternoon, and many of the members had left the floor, there being only 39 present out of a total of 116. This constituted a quorum under the rules of the House, but it was hardly representative.

Henry had seven resolves, all against the Stamp Act, denying the right of Parliament to impose such a measure upon the colonies. He read them one by one, and they were voted upon separately. They got more outspoken as they went along, and the fifth squeezed through by only a single vote, 19 to 20. After that Mr. Henry decided to keep the other two in his pocket, though he seems to have handed copies of them around or put them into the record.

"By God, I would have given five hundred guineas for a single vote," Peyton Randolph stormed as he came, steaming, out of the chamber after the vote on the fifth resolve.[19] He meant of course that in the case of a tie the ultra-conservative speaker, John Robinson, would have voted the resolve out. It was quashed the next day anyway, expunged from the record, though the first four remained.

The official printer, Joseph Royle of the *Virginia Gazette*, flatly refused to print even the first four resolves, which he thought treasonous. Somehow, though, perhaps by mail, copies of *all seven*, not just the first four, reached ardent Whigs in Philadelphia and were passed from hand to hand, it being understood, at least for a long while, that all seven of them had been passed by the Virginia House of Burgesses. Then somebody sent a set of them to the radical editor of the Newport, R.I., *Mercury*, which published them June 24; and the fat was in the fire.

6

THE TAINT OF ENGLISHNESS

THE *Boston Gazette* printed the complete Patrick Henry resolutions July 2, and this caused a stir. "They are men," cried the ailing Oxenbridge Thacher. "They are noble spirits!" Then he died; but the cause he had represented so vehemently did not die, but rather swelled like a flood, sweeping the land. Committees met; messengers galloped; militiamen marched back and forth, muskets on their shoulders; and there was a rash of speech-making and resolution-passing, while the members of the Virginia House of Burgesses, to their own astonishment, were hailed as heroes.

Boston had not been idle. Even before the news from Williamsburg arrived, the Massachusetts General Court, on June 6, had voted to consider a plan to appoint a committee to confer with similar committees from other colonies on what might be done about the Stamp Act. On June 8 the Court issued a circular letter to the legislatures of all twelve other colonies proposing a general meeting in New York the second Tuesday in October. Precisely what the men in Whitehall feared was about to happen. The colonies were getting together.

To all of this Governor Bernard objected, but it did him no good. The four members of the "Boston seat," radicals, were firmly in command of the lower house, and they meant to catch up with and to pass the Burgesses of Virginia. James Otis was elected speaker, and when Bernard refused to approve this election—as he had a right to do, though it was only the second time in the history of the Massachusetts Bay colony that any governor had done this—the House elected an only slightly less violent Whig, Thomas Cushing. Samuel Adams, by one vote, was elected clerk of the House; and about this election the Governor had nothing, legally, to say.

It was Sam Adams who framed the circular letter calling for a Stamp Act congress, and this might be a good time to take a better look at him.

His father, one of the founders of the Caucus Club, had left him a maltery, but young Sam, who at one time had studied a little law, at another time a little theology, soon had the business bankrupt. He just could not be bothered. Politics was all that interested him. His friends got him a job as, of all things, tax collector. As anybody who knew him could have predicted, Sam Adams soon made a hash of this. He wasn't dishonest! Nobody ever accused him of dishonesty. He was just appallingly inefficient. When he learned that his accounts were some £7,000 in arrears he simply could not understand where the money had gone. Despite sundry court actions, he never was called upon to pay any of this back, for the man had, besides an abiding faith in the American people, many, many friends. Thomas Hutchinson, who abhorred him, was wont to refer to Samuel Adams' "defalcations," but not even Hutchinson would contend that he had spent any money on *himself*.

The house he had inherited in Purchase Street was a large one. It soon was in ruins, for Sam was too busy politicking to make any repairs. His first wife died, leaving him two small children, and he married again. There was also a Negro slave girl and a Newfoundland dog, and many a time they did not have enough to eat; but this never fazed Sam Adams; and neighbors would send things in.

He was an old-line Puritan, austere in his habits—family prayers every weekday, Bible readings at night, twice to church on Sunday. He never seemed to sleep. He knew everybody. He got everywhere.

Hutchinson, who hated *him* too, once said of James Otis that he was "more fit for a madhouse than the House of Representatives," a rather unfortunate remark, as the event proved, since Otis did in fact die a committed lunatic. Nobody would have said such a thing of Samuel Adams, who could make an impromptu speech on any occasion but who had none of the inspired eloquence of Otis, the appeal of young Josiah Quincy, Jr., the dignity of Dr. Joseph Warren, that persuasive macaroni-physician who was to lay down his life at Bunker Hill, nor yet the hardheaded logic of his own second cousin, John Adams, a lawyer from Braintree, who likewise was looming large in the patriot cause. Sam Adams tended to rant, and to repeat himself. He got shrill. But he drove himself without mercy. He never hesitated or took a backward step. He got many of his effects by sheer persistence, by refusing to take no for an answer, a system practiced by many more recent purveyors of propaganda.

He had a nice sense of words. As clerk of the General Court he always referred to the Town House or Court House—it was called both—as the *State* House, thereby infuriating Thomas Hutchinson. He would refer, too, to the "Parliamentary" debates that were held there, and to the "Parliamentary" decisions reached by "his Majesty's Commons," assuming a sovereignty the General Court surely never

105   From the *Magazine of American History*, Vol. I, 1877, copy of a handbill
preserved in the State Paper Office, London

3. A HANDBILL PROTESTING THE USE OF STAMPS

had possessed, though it sometimes acted as if it did. Another trick of this tricky man was to refer to the Massachusetts Bay Charter, which the Governor and the Lieutenant Governor though of as a gracious royal grant, as the "compact," implying that King and Commonwealth, as equal partners, had reached a mutual agreement.

He was even more effective in print. He wrote as he spoke, pauselessly and with great earnestness; but he wrote better than he spoke, and he developed a clear, unornamented style. Besides all of his official correspondence he exchanged regular letters, always on political matters, with prominent Whigs elsewhere in the colony and in other colonies and even in England. Then too, he wrote voluminously for newspapers, using, as was the custom, classical pen names, over twenty of which have been traced to him.[20] His wife would tell of waking in the middle of the night and seeing the light still coming from a candle in Samuel's ramshackle study, from whence came too the untiring scratch of Samuel's pen, hour after hour.

The copies of the official portrait of Samuel Adams that hang in numberless schools and state houses throughout the land are just that—official. He had been dressed for the sitting, no doubt in borrowed clothes. He was a man of medium height and with a slight pot belly. His eyes were gray and his hair was graying, though he was in no sense an *eminence gris*, being much too voluble. His hands shook with palsy and his lips twitched most of the time. His voice was reedy and high. But—he knew what he wanted.

The more folks thought about this Stamp Act business the more they resented it. Some, perhaps many, were less interested in the technical difference, if any, between an external tax and an internal tax or the right or lack of right of Parliament to impose any sort of impost upon a people who were not represented on the floor of Commons, than they were interested in the immediate financial impact such a law would make. It was provided that all stamped paper must be paid for in cash, of which there was precious little in the colonies, it being a time of post-war slump, and the penalties for violation, which must also be paid in cash, were heavy.

It would cost a student £2 to enter a university, another £2 to be graduated. Admission to the bar (it was only £6 under the stamp act in effect in England) would be £10, an enormous sum which would undoubtedly have ruled out many a talented youngster—John Adams, for example, and Patrick Henry. Young couples about to get married were notoriously in need of money, but under the Stamp Act they would have £2 more added to the demands upon them, that being the proposed tax on a license.

Three of the most powerful classes of men in the American colonies were the newspaper publishers—or printers, as they were always called and as in fact they usually were—the tavern keepers, and the attorneys.

There were a great many newspapers in the colonies, most of them liberal weeklies, and almost to a roller, even the conservative ones, they opposed the Stamp Act, which would have raised their price and lowered their circulation.

The publican was to be charged only £1 a year, but this could be a crushing fee to a man who was in the business only in a small way, perhaps part-time. The village dispenser of ale, wine, rum, and applejack, was more than just a bung-starter. He was a counsellor, a moderator, often even an oracle. And what *he* thought of the Stamp Act could not be said in the presence of females.

The colonists were the most cantankerous and most contentious people on earth, forever suing one another, haling one another into court. They cursed their lawyers, who were many, but at the same time they loved them. Yet if they were to have to pay a duty on every legal paper issued they would soon learn to settle their differences less formally, and then how would the lawyers eat? The lawyers viewed with a great deal of alarm the approach of Stamp Act Day, November 1.

Grenville had studied the situation, and he knew that the American colonists disliked "foreigners"—even though they came from England—who arrived in their midst with the obligation to collect something, to enforce something. General Gage was married to a New Jersey woman, but even so he and his redcoats in New York, a mere handful—most of the British Army forces on the continent were in Nova Scotia or the Floridas [21]—were hooted when they appeared in the streets. The royal governors, the lieutenant governors as well, might be personally well-liked, but politically they were, most of them, anathema. Admiralty court judges were feared. Customs officers were despised.

Grenville planned to offset this aversion to outside collectors by providing that the distributors appointed under the Stamp Act be, as often as possible (and Georgia was the only colony in which he could find nobody), residents of the colony in which they were to work. He reasoned that it would be easier to pay a neighbor than a "foreigner." It would take the taint of Englishness from the deal.

These so-called stamp masters were to be paid £300 a year, a sum not princely perhaps but pleasant, and the position was rated "genteel." It could be a sinecure: any needy clerk of tolerable intelligence would be glad to do all the paper work for a third of that sum.

Benjamin Franklin, in London, thought so well of the prospects of these new posts that he named a couple of candidates of his own—Jared Ingersoll in Connecticut, John Hughes in Pennsylvania, who, thanks to the good doctor's influence, were appointed. Franklin had worked hard against the passage of the Stamp Act, but once it *had been* passed he saw no reason why he should not get jobs for a couple of friends. He really thought that he was doing them a favor. In fact he was ruining their political careers.

Richard Henry Lee, member of a famous family and perhaps for that reason a mite removed from the ruck of mankind, actually put in for the mastership of stamps in Virginia; and he probably would have got it, too, had he not realized just in time what a hot potato he was holding, and dropped it.

Fervent protestations of loyalty to His Gracious Majesty the King, well-thought-out arguments against the right of Parliament to impose internal taxes upon the unrepresented colonies, alike went to waste. They were not studied, and in many cases were not even read. The matter, then, called for more direct action.

It was apparent that if there were no distributors of stamps there would be no distribution, and if there was no distribution there would be no *use* of stamps. The best thing to do would be burn the stamps, but this might be difficult if they were protected by the military, and anyway more could be sent from England. The next best thing—and the surest, most immediate thing—was to persuade the stamp masters to resign, even before the stamps arrived. If a substitute was promptly appointed, that substitute too could be persuaded, orally if possible, physically if necessary, to refuse to accept the post. Only a few examples would be needed, it was believed. The remaining appointees would soon see the light.

Now this was work that printers and lawyers, and even the more placid of the publicans, might hesitate to do. It was, however, work for which the Sons of Liberty were well qualified, as they were presently to prove.

AN EXPRESSION

OF DISAPPROVAL

O N THE MORNING of August 14 those who lived in the vicinity of the Liberty Tree in King Street, Boston,[22] rose to see dangling from that landmark a crude effigy, and fastened to this were an old jackboot, something that was generally taken to be a devil with stamps in its hand, and a sign reading that this, the effigy proper, represented Andrew Oliver.

It made sense to the Bostonians. It meant that Mackintosh, the flint-fisted cobbler who headed the South End "chickens," had paid the Tree a visit, and that trouble could be expected soon.

Oliver was a brother-in-law of Thomas Hutchinson, the lieutenant governor, and he was not well-liked. A rich, reserved man who had little respect for what he sometimes called the *mob*ility, he was secretary of the colony—that is to say, the number three man—and from time to time he or some of his relatives held other positions in the Massachusetts government. This was not an uncommon condition—nepotism was much more flagrant in New Hampshire, for example, where virtually *every* public servant was a Wentworth—but it did not make for goodwill on the part of the disappointed office seekers, the men Hutchinson had called "canker-worms of the State." What's more—and here an ominous note was sounded—Oliver, it had recently been whispered, would get the appointment as stamp master of Massachusetts. This report had not yet been confirmed, but "the First Captain-General of the Liberty Tree" and his thugs were not interested in confirmation.

Governor Bernard ordered the effigy cut down, but soon the sheriff came to him and said that he would be risking his own life and the lives of his deputies if he took any such action.

So there it stayed, all day.

At nightfall, as expected, the ruffians assembled there. They cut the effigy down. They bore it to the building Andrew Oliver was putting up on his dock at the foot of Kilby Street, which building they had heard was to be used as the stamp office. (This was not true: Oliver had only intended it for shops, as a speculation.) They pulled the building apart and carried the wooden portions of it up to the top of nearby Beacon Hill, where they made a bonfire of them and beheaded and burned the effigy.

Then they started for Andrew Oliver's house. Hutchinson and the sheriff intercepted them and tried to talk them into subsiding, but these two were showered with stones and had to beat a retreat.

Oliver had been warned. The house was empty. The gangsters went through it like a swarm of locusts, smashing all the windows, smashing everything smashable, including what was reputed to be the largest looking glass in North America. Not until then did they disperse.

The next day Andrew Oliver publicly promised to resign, once he was appointed. And when the expected commission did arrive he was required to resign all over again, at the

Liberty Tree before a jeering crowd. He was glad to get out of it that easily.

His brother-in-law was not so fortunate. Two days after the attack on Oliver's house Hutchinson's house was fronted by a catcalling crowd. A few rocks were thrown, but there was no concerted attack. That was to wait until August 26, a night that Boston would long remember.

Rumors flew all over town the day of August 26 that there would be some real action that night, and a bonfire before the Town House in King Street right after sundown summoned the faithful, who in a little while broke into two parties.

One of these plundered and wrecked the elegant new house of Benjamin Hallowell, the comptroller of customs, whose cellar was well stocked with wine. Nobody tried to restrain them.

The other mob descended upon the home of Charles Paxton, marshal of the court of vice-admiralty, who, keeping his head, talked them into adjourning to a nearby bar, where he bought them a whole barrel of punch. They left him alone after that.

From the tavern, the second mob, led by Mackintosh in person, visited the home of William Story, the register of the vice-admiralty court. There they first made a fire of all the court papers they could find, and then wrecked the house.

Now the two mobs came together, seemingly by pre-arrangement, and surged toward Thomas Hutchinson's large square white house in Garden Court Street.

Hutchinson at sixty-two was not a man to scare easily. It was still early, and he was at supper when he heard about the mob. He knew that despite his record of opposition to the Stamp Act it was generally supposed, among the great unwashed, that he secretly favored it, and indeed the rumor had been spread that Thomas Hutchinson had actually *conceived* and *written* the Stamp Act right here in this handsome house.

So they were coming for him, were they? He sent the servants and all members of his family out the back way, telling them where to go for safety, where to lie low. He himself proposed to stay right where he was.

Even when the mob got close he did not stir. He had barricaded the door, and he stood just inside of it, his jaw jutting. It was not until his eldest daughter came back, and tugged at him, and vowed that if he would not run she would stay right there with him, that he agreed to bolt.

He was just in time. That daughter undoubtedly saved his life.

As a matter of mere routine, a warming-up, the mob smashed all the front windows first. Then with axes it battered down the fine polished mahogany doors. It smashed all the side and back windows, upstairs and down. After that it went mad.

This was the work of fiends. Nothing was spared. Tapestries and paintings were slashed. Linen was ripped, the very mattresses reduced to ribbons. Clothing was torn and tossed about. The stairposts were splintered. Cash to the amount of £900 was stolen, as was some of the furniture, though most of the pieces of stolen furniture were later found abandoned, hacked to pieces, in the streets. Some of the men tumbled into the garden, there to uproot all the bushes and chop down the trees. Some burst into the Lieutenant-Governor's library and defaced his books and scooped up and carried outside his papers, irreplaceable papers, papers he had spent thirty years collecting, together with the manuscript of the second volume of his *History of the Province of Massachusetts Bay*. These, luckily, they did not burn. They only dumped them into the street, into the mud.[23]

The kitchen utensils were stolen, the china, every single piece of it, reduced to dust.

This took some time, and it took a great deal of energy, but the wreckers were not yet through. They battered down the partitions between rooms. They climbed to the roof and tried to tear off the huge round cupola that surmounted the house, and when they could not budge this they started to rip off the roof itself, which was made of slate.

The dawn found them thus employed. But they didn't like daylight, and scuttled away.

"Such ruins were never seen in America," Hutchinson wrote to a friend.[24]

There was a great outcry, and it seems to have been sincere. No doubt many of the men who deplored the deed so loudly had known what was going to happen and had aided and abetted it, on the quiet; but now they were shocked by the extent of the damage, the ferocity of the attack. They had not known that it would go so far.

There were all sorts of resolutions of regret and indignation. The General Court itself passed such a resolution. The General Court went further and accepted Thomas Hutchinson's petition for indemnity, granting him exactly what he had asked, £3,194 17s. 6d. However, there was a rider to this grant: nobody might be prosecuted for the attack. Governor Bernard signed it reluctantly, knowing that if he did not his friend would get nothing at all. King George, months later, disallowed this grant with its shameful condition.[25] His majesty said that he was sorry for Mr. Hutchinson, who should certainly be reimbursed, but he could not countenance such a precedent. It did no good. By that time the money had been paid and everybody was trying to forget it.

The result would have been the same anyway. The result would have been—no legal action. Mackintosh, who openly boasted about his part in the affair, was arrested next day, but he was held only a few hours. Half a dozen others were taken in, but they were not held long. No charges were lodged against anybody.

The very next night, after the wrecking of the Hutchinson house—though it is unlikely that the news had reached Rhode Island by that time—was a somewhat similar night-of-mobs at Newport.

Rhode Island, following publication of the Virginia Resolves, had been one of the loudest of those in protest against both the impending Stamp Act and the already-a-fact Sugar Act, but in particular the latter, since so much of the colony's livelihood was involved in illegal trade. They, alone among the thirteen colonies, actually promised to indemnify anybody who lost property or was hurt *resisting* either of these acts.

On the night of August 27, then, Augustus Johnston was forced to resign as stamp master, though like Oliver in Boston he had not yet been commissioned. John Robinson, the collector of customs, took refuge aboard of a British war vessel, *Cygnet*. Then, while the sheriff sat tight and the Governor prudently left town, the mob addressed itself to the fine homes of two men who had dared to write in favor of the Stamp Act, Martin Howard, a lawyer, and a physician, Dr. Thomas Moffat, whose residence was especially desirable because of its well-stocked cellar. In each case a thorough job was done; and nobody was arrested.

So it went everywhere, though in other places there was less violence, the mere threat ordinarily being enough. McEvers in New York, Ingersoll in Connecticut, Hughes in Pennsylvania, ringingly resigned. George Meserve of New Hampshire, returning from a visit to England with his commission as stamp master in his pocket, was handed a letter by the pilot, before he even landed, a letter in which sundry important New Hampshire officials pleaded that he resign immediately for the sake of the public peace; and this he did. George Mercer of Virginia, Caleb Lloyd and George Saxby of the Carolinas, George Angus, the only Englishman, who was to have taken over the stamps in Georgia, saw the light and signed their resignations. One, Zachariah Hood of Maryland, fought—for a little while. Lucky to have the clothes he stood in, he escaped to New York; but there the local members of the Sons of Liberty, in an act of co-operation that must have been without precedent, forced his resignation from him—and so notified the Maryland organization.

America, it might be said, had expressed its disapproval of the Stamp Act.

CHAPTER

8

DON'T LOOK AT IT

THERE WAS SOMETHING the matter with the King.
Perhaps it was pleurisy, perhaps only a bad cold. Popular
report, in later years, had it that this illness early in 1765 was
the first outcropping of those fits of madness that were to
darken the latter part of the royal life;[26] but no idea of this
appears to have been entertained at the time; and when the
ministers gathered for the purpose of agreeing upon a board
of regency, lest the King's illness prove more serious than it
then seemed, it was only with the thought of death, not the
thought of insanity. The board was to be similar to those that
had functioned during the reigns of the first two Georges,
who hated England and lost no opportunity to scamper back
to their beloved Hanover. *Somebody* had to be authorized to
sign for them, in their absence. George III's children, at the
time, were tiny. Without such a board there would be great
confusion in the event of his death. So the board of regency
was appointed.

George Grenville voted against inclusion in it of the
King's mother, the dowager Princess of Wales; and when the

King, recovered, heard of this, he was furious, for he assumed, perhaps rightly, perhaps wrongly, that Grenville's objection to the Princess lay in his belief in the old story about her being Bute's mistress. He turned against Grenville, whom he had never liked anyway; and the cabinet fell.

This happened in July, before the fiasco of Stamp Act enforcement had become known, indeed before it had fully happened. Grenville's group might have lasted at least another six months, or even more. Without the support of the King's Men, that little gang of obedient employees herded by the ubiquitous Bute, it could not last an hour.

It was replaced by a cabinet headed by the Marquis of Rockingham, "a dyspeptic and somewhat querulous young man," [27] who was on the whole thought to be slightly gentler than Grenville in his views of the American colonies.

"Pretty summer wear," was what "Champagne Charlie" Townshend said of the Rockingham group, "but it will never stand the winter." He called it "a lute string cabinet." This was the same bright young man who had provoked the "sons of liberty" retort from Colonel Barré; and he was wrong again, for the Rockingham cabinet lasted a whole year, until the following July.

Having got rid of the stamp masters, the colonists, while they waited to see what an enraged mother country would do about it, proceeded to discuss plans for getting rid of the stamps.

This proved to be a problem that solved itself. The first stamps to arrive were destined for Massachusetts, Rhode Island, and New Hampshire. They came to Boston. Not only was there nobody to distribute them: there was nobody to receive them, accept them, sign for them. The Massachusetts stamps were stored at Fort William for safekeeping; the others were taken to a couple of warships anchored in the bay; and there they all remained.

Much the same procedure was followed in other ports. Somebody at Home had been remiss, and official copies of the Stamp Act did not arrive in several of the colonies until the last minute—and in at least one, Georgia, not until *after* that last minute. This formed a convenient excuse for doing nothing.

The telling time, the deadline, would be November 1, when the Act was supposed to go into effect. Meanwhile lawyers and judges were hurrying their cases, and ships' masters were loading their cargo with all convenient speed.

The Stamp Act Congress, which met at New York in October, was not much immediate help. It was a serious sober body, consisting of twenty-seven delegates from nine of the thirteen colonies. New Hampshire declined an invitation to attend but later approved the proceedings. The Virginia, North Carolina, and Georgia legislatures could not appoint delegates because the several royal governors refused to convene them for that purpose. The same thing applied to Delaware and New Jersey, but there many members of the legislature got together and appointed their own slates of delegates. This procedure was of course illegal, but then the whole Congress was illegal, or at least extra-legal, anyway.

The tone of the Congress was notably moderate. Two of the three Massachusetts delegates, James Otis and an arch-conservative, Timothy Ruggles, were proposed for the chairmanship; Ruggles won readily. True, Otis, at the moment, was in one of his more quiescent moods—nobody ever knew what he would do next—but still, his name was so closely associated with radicalism that the Stamp Act Congress shied away from him. An effort on the part of the South Carolina delegates, headed by Christopher Gadsden, to provide a "broader base" for the protest than mere charter privileges, was easily defeated, another victory of conservatism. The chairman, General Ruggles, at the end of two weeks of discussion—no detail of which ever was made public—refused to sign or in any way certify the resolutions at last adopted. For this he was reproved by his own legislature.

The resolutions were thirteen in number, together with a preamble and an afterword, all, almost certainly, written by John Dickinson of Philadelphia. They were warm yet not suspiciously hot in their protestations of loyalty to King and Crown, and in acknowledgment of the supreme power of Parliament; but they remained firm—and in this they undoubtedly reflected the thinking of a majority of Americans at the time—in their assertion that even Parliament could not impose an internal tax upon the colonies when the said colonies were not in any way represented in the said Parliament.

It was little enough, perhaps, but it was a dignified document, and well written. It was to be sent, along with separate petitions, to the King, the House of Lords, and the House of Commons. These petitions would not be considered, of course. It was likely that they would not even be read. That was not important. What *was* important was that the American colonies for the first time had got together for a serious, sane, even-tempered discussion of their troubles. There would, surely, be more such meetings.

American merchants took a different course. It was not predetermined, and it had nothing to do with the Sons of Liberty or any other activist organization. Indeed, it seems to have been prompted by trepidation rather than boldness. The merchants stopped paying their bills abroad.

The merchants, it was estimated, owed their British associates about £4,000,000. At a time like this, when almost anything, even war, might happen at almost any moment, they were understandably reluctant to let metal money get out of their hands. It was not a concerted movement calculated to intimidate, but simple business caution. The British merchants, many of them already over-extended, squawked loudly. They picked up their pens and wrote to people they knew in Parliament. John Dickinson's mannered, elegantly framed resolutions might go unread in English high places, but those letters from the merchants of London, Bristol, and Liverpool would not.

As the great day approached there were all sorts of rumors, but then it passed off quietly enough. Everywhere flags were at half-mast and church bells were tolled—lugubriously, not gaily—but the only violence was in New York that night, when a mob burned the lieutenant governor's coach and looted the home of the highly unpopular commanding officer, a major, who was safe in Fort George at the time. New York always had been a rough place.

At first, along the waterfronts, it made little difference, except that there were fewer ships in port than usual; many skippers had cleared out just under the wire, while those who were still loading in many cases had anticipatory clearances dated October 31. Soon, however, the anchorages and the wharf spaces began to fill with vessels, while at the same time the ports began to fill with idle sailors, always a bad condition. Once these sailors had drunk up their wages—and that never took long—they would be faced with starvation. And why? Who was keeping them from work, from food? Only the King's precious customs officers, who refused to issue papers without stamps. There was a nasty mutter. The Sons of Liberty would get many a recruit here.

There was a great deal of buck-passing in official circles and all sorts of excuses for inaction were made, but sooner or later the matter had to come to a head. First here, then there, and at last all up and down the whole thirteen colonies, the customs men, frankly fearful of their lives, began to issue clearances—on unstamped paper. In many cases these were accompanied by letters explaining to whom it may concern that there *were* no stamps. It was hoped that these would pre-vail. Yankee ingenuity being what it was, there were soon special insurance policies being written against the possibility of seizure by naval officers, who, to incite their fervor, were offered a split of the prize. These policies, expensive at first, soon settled back to 2½ per cent, which nobody minded paying.

The navy men, as it turned out, were not remarkably active. They were no longer sure of themselves, for the Stamp Act itself, or rather the unexpectedly stiff resistance to it, was cramping them. The Stamp Act did not interfere with crim-inal courts, but it did apply to civil courts and to vice-admiralty courts. These were now closed. A seized vessel and its cargo would have to be sent all the way to Halifax, where there was a vice-admiralty court that used stamped paper; but this court, of course, was heavily overcrowded and it might take months, even a year or more, to get a condemnation. So the navy men were waiting until the whole situation could be clarified, and this brought the insurance rates down.

Soon all the American ports were buzzing with activity, though the American merchants still were not paying their debts to British merchants, since for *that* they would need stamped paper—and they did not have stamped paper.

Getting the courts open took longer, perhaps because of the innate conservatism of the legal mind. But it was done—not all at once, not in a rush, but slowly, apologetically, and by force of circumstances.

By the end of the year the American colonies were re-porting business as usual, or a little better than that. They had circumvented the Stamp Act by the simple process of ignoring it. Don't look at it (was the declared attitude) and it will go away.

It was not likely that Great Britain would agree.

9

THE GREAT DEBATE

IN THE CHRISTMAS RECESS of Parliament some of the more influential ministers met at the London home of the Marquis of Rockingham in order to talk about what, if anything, they should do. Present were General Conway, secretary of state for the Southern Department, which, strangely enough, included America; Charles Yorke, the attorney general; William Dowdeswell, chancellor of the exchequer; the Earl of Egmont, first lord of the admiralty; Lord Dartmouth, president of the Board of Trade; and the petulant marquis himself. None of them ever had set foot in America; but then, their problem was not geographical but political. For they faced a crisis. The speech from the throne had made mention of "many inconveniences" in the administration of the Stamp Act, which was a masterpiece of understatement. The ministers assembled at the marquis's home knew how serious the situation was. It could be that others did too; and if they did not know, inevitably they soon would. The ministers must be ready for this.

Several courses were considered. The first was an old-fashioned resort to the sword. Send over the Army! send over the Navy! and say to the colonists: Damn it, you obey this law or else! This was soon rejected, General Conway being especially vehement in opposition to it. Such behavior would be unnatural, pitting brother, as it were, against brother; it would be unpopular; it would be expensive. What was more, it would do nothing to relieve the distress of those English merchants who were weeping about—and writing about—the loss of their American trade. It would do nothing about paying off that £4,000,000 debt.

Or, the ministers could emulate the colonists and pretend that the Stamp Act never had existed. This was unthinkable. It would be an open confession that the most powerful nation in history could not enforce its own commands at home. It would be an invitation to the American colonists, new and old, to try it again. It would be a suggestion that the West Indians and the other far-flung colonists, in time no doubt even the *East* Indians, might tell the mother country to go to Hell any time they felt like it. This would never do.

The men at the marquis's had no love for the Stamp Act, which they had not originated, only inherited; and if they could use this impasse as a stick with which to belabor George Grenville, why, that would be fine. Grenville was leading the opposition now, and he would certainly take a strong line in defense of the act with which his name was ineradicably and quite properly linked.

It was agreed, first of all—and this was almost the only thing that *was* agreed—that the colonists must be put sharply and emphatically into their place. They should be told, in no uncertain tones, that the British Parliament was supreme over everything within the British Empire, and a law should be enacted making it high treason to question this. Once this chore had been attended to, the Stamp Act might, after all, be somewhat modified. Since the colonists had made such a fuss about it, maybe there was something inherently wrong in the thing? Perhaps the duties on ships' cockets and clearances should be greatly reduced, or even done away with? Perhaps the colonists would be quiet if the act permitted payment in the local currency, instead of insisting upon sterling? or if the fines for failure to pay were reduced? or if violations were tried in the courts of record, which had juries, instead of the vice-admiralty courts, which did not? Each of these possibilities was discussed, and each had proponents; but each had opponents as well; and in the end the conference settled upon nothing except a very general strategy. In effect, it purposed to dump the whole matter back into the lap of Parliament. This was not a strong government.

So much depended upon Pitt! The Great Commoner at this time might have been called the Great Question Mark. Nobody knew where he stood, and it is quite possible that he didn't know himself. In wartime he had been magnificent, a dynamo. The thing to do with a war, he had reasoned, was win it. In peace time he remained personally sensational, a great orator, adored on both sides of the sea; but he had no party behind him, and so no power, except for that which his prestige lent him. His followers were few: long on talent, they were short in numbers. Even they did not know what to expect of him. They loved him as a person, not necessarily as a leader. He was in poor health, and for days on end, for weeks, he would see no one for more than a few minutes at a time and would answer no questions. He had taken no part in the passage of the Stamp Act, and so had no vote on record.

George III, like his grandfather before him, hated and feared William Pitt, who scolded him, bullied him, and made speeches at him that the poor bewildered monarch could not understand. All the same, when the Grenville cabinet fell

King George perforce turned to Pitt, who thereupon began to dictate his terms, for Pitt never would play on any team of which he was not the captain, and he insisted upon writing the rules of the game in advance. "I am sure I can save this country, and nobody else can," he had announced at the beginning of the Seven Years' War; and this still was his stand. Rockingham, then, got the job. Even the King could only stand so much.

The flashing eyes, the hawklike, imperious nose of the Great Commoner had not been seen in the House for many months, and the great, rich, utterly-sure-of-itself, scornful voice had not been raised. But he made it, somehow, this time, dramatizing his physical weakness, when the House was reconvened after the Christmas recess. And he spoke.

Rather, he erupted. Like some glorious volcano, eager to prove that it really was not extinct, he poured forth steam and hissing, polychromatic lava, together with sparks that lighted the sky for miles around. He blistered, he scalded. But if he was not always consistent, at least William Pitt never failed to be positive; and now he left no doubt as to what he thought of the Stamp Act.

"I rejoice that America has resisted," he cried. "The gentleman asks, when were the colonies emancipated? But I desire to know, when were they made slaves? . . . Upon the whole, I will beg leave to tell the House what is really my opinion. It is, that the Stamp Act be repealed absolutely, totally, and immediately."

It was a great speech, even for him, one of his most memorable. It was coruscating, it was brilliant, sublime. It left the members stunned; and it might even have changed a few votes.

Pitt did more than make a mighty speech for repeal of the Stamp Act. Again and again he called for a reading before the House of the various petitions sent in by the colonies and by the Stamp Act Congress. This was refused, on technical grounds. Not that there was any lack of petitions! The Rockingham ministry, sometimes called the Old Whigs, lacking a clear majority in Parliament and being unsure of the support of the King's Men, had turned to the merchants, who had welcomed it with gusto. The trade with America was not getting better, as some had hoped, but worse—very much worse. Merchants in Philadelphia, Boston, New York, all up and down the mainland, sober men, responsible men, not members of mobs, had solemnly pledged themselves to buy nothing from England that was not vitally needed until such time as the Stamp Act had been repealed. Even merchants of the West Indies were in arms against the Stamp Act. The Sugar Act aided them, as opposed to the mainlanders, whom it hurt; but the Stamp Act hurt both; and the Sugar Aristocrats were against it to a man.

4. THE HATED STAMP

The debate at the time of passage of this disputed Act had been perfunctory. The debate over its repeal was anything but that. The Commons heard scores of merchants, bankers, businessmen. They even heard a few Americans, among whom Benjamin Franklin was the star. Franklin jolted the members when he denied that the Seven Years' War was a gallant protective struggle for the sake of the American colonies.

"I know the last war is commonly spoken of here as entered into for the defence, or for the sake of the people of America. I think it is quite misunderstood. . . . We had therefore no particular concern or interest in the dispute. . . . It was not until after his [Braddock's] defeat that the colonies were attacked. They were before in perfect peace with both French and Indians. . . ."

Franklin's most telling point was an insistence that the colonies objected only to internal as distinguished from external taxation. He hammered this, and it was effective.

Pitt, for his part, made the rather curious assertion that taxation was not part of legislation. The British Parliament, he argued, had supreme legislative power over the colonies, but this did not include taxation. He clashed on this point, publicly and shrilly, with his brother-in-law, George Grenville.

The internal-external distinction bobbed up again in the discussion of the Declaratory Act, which it was planned would precede any action on repeal, and which did not, after all, contain any mention of high treason. Rockingham himself, who framed the thing, was careful to keep out of it any reference to taxation, lest Pitt's feelings be hurt. What he wrote was: "The King's Majesty, by and with the advice of the lords spiritual and temporal, and commons of Great Britain, in Parliament assembled, had, hath, and of right ought to have, full force and validity to bind the colonies and people of America, subjects of the Crown of Great Britain, in all cases whatsoever."

This the marquis thought strong enough, and he submitted it to his attorney general, Charles Yorke, a man he did not get along well with, for an opinion. Yorke suggested that the end be changed to "as well in cases of Taxation, as in all other cases whatsoever," but Rockingham, still thinking of Pitt, vetoed this.

When the Declaratory Act was submitted on the floor Colonel Barré moved an amendment to strike out the words "in all cases whatsoever," and Pitt seconded this, while in the Peers Camden was moving the same amendment. It was lost in both houses.

This prepared the way for the great debate on repeal, which ended at two o'clock of the morning of Saturday, February 22—the House of Commons had been in session since ten o'clock the previous morning—with a vote of 275 to 167 in favor of repeal.

10

IT HAD BEEN A NEAR THING

GLAD AS THEY WERE, the colonists did not gloat. In England merchant after tremulous merchant, fearful that they *would* gloat, seized his pen and implored American correspondents to refrain from over-exuberance of celebration in connection with the repeal of the Stamp Act. Repeal, they averred, had been accomplished not because of but in spite of the riots and the protests, dignified and otherwise, which indeed had postponed it. Any evidence on the part of the Americans that they thought they had browbeaten Parliament into retracting its words might well be fatal to the colonial hopes. There were those in England, the merchants wrote, who feared just that, and who at the first sign of colonial strutting might well set about working for the *re-enactment* of the Stamp Act. So—let the Americans be circumspect.

George Mason of Virginia was not amused. The English merchants, he wrote to a friend, seemed to be saying: "We have with infinite difficulty and fatigue got you excused this one time; pray be a good boy for the future, do what your papa and mama bid you, and hasten to return them your most

grateful acknowledgments for condescending to let you keep
what is your own; and then all your acquaintance will love
you, and praise you, and will give you pretty things. . . .

"Is not this a little ridiculous," he went on, "when applied to three millions of as loyal and useful subjects as any
in the British dominions, who have been only contending for
their birth-right, and have now only gained, or rather kept,
what could not, with common justice, or even policy, be
denied them?" [28]

The English merchants might have spared themselves the
trouble. Their own countrymen had made a great to-do at
the news of the Stamp Act repeal, for it was widely thought in
England that the tax had been responsible for hard times, and
with the repeal employment figures shot up; but the Americans, two months later, received the news with what in the
circumstances might be rated as a rare composure. There were
toasts, to be sure; there were speeches, some of them perfervid;
there were even a few parades. Pitt, long a favorite on both
sides of the sea, was hailed as a hero, the man who almost
single-handedly had righted a great wrong, and in New York
the citizenry raised funds for a gigantic lead equestrian statue
of King George, who likewise was much praised for the part
he had played.[29] On the whole the news was received in the
colonies with an absence of the wild joy that had marked its
reception in England. It had been a near thing. Americans
were sobered to see how close they had come to the hot con-
suming breath of war.

The Americans were under no illusion. They knew that it
had not been a triumph of justice and right over the forces of
evil. They knew that their prayers and petitions had *in themselves* gone unheeded, and that what had counted most in
causing Parliament to rescind the Stamp Act was not the truth
of the continental cause, not a regard for the constitutional
rights of Englishmen who happened to live three thousand

miles from Home, but the noise made by the English merchants. John Bull had been hit in his most vulnerable spot—the pocketbook. That £4,000,000 debt swung more votes than all the resolutions and well-reasoned arguments put together. Nevertheless it could not be denied that the English merchants would not have moved if the colonists had not done so first. Had the colonists submitted to what a majority of them sincerely believed was an unfair tax would the manufacturers of Leeds and the exporters of London suddenly see the light? It was unlikely, to say the least. And when all was said and done, when distinctions between internal and external taxes were over and forgotten, and the last echo of the last resounding speech had frittered itself away in a remote small corner, the simple fact remained that the American colonists and the mother country had clashed—and the mother country had given in. The colonists might not gloat about this, but they would not forget it.

The business had made a profound difference in America. It had taught the colonies, rather to their own astonishment, that they could work together.[30] It had greatly enhanced the prestige of the Sons of Liberty and such extremists as James Otis and Patrick Henry, while moderates like John Hughes and Jared Ingersoll, men who might have helped to avert a real clash, were cast into a political obscurity from which they were never to emerge. It had set men to thinking. "Independence" no longer was a dirty word.

Austerity too played a part. Moralists were pleased, as well as the politically radical; and even though after repeal there was a relapse into luxury, the colonists had shown what they could do when they had to. The great non-importation agreements were the work of merchants in the cities, but there were many other changes and they came from humbler sources.

The pretentious, crushingly expensive funerals and

mourning customs in fashion at the time were forsworn for a more sensible procedure. Thousands not kept in line by the Liberty Boys had signed agreements not to eat lamb until the Stamp Act was repealed, the idea being to keep the animals alive until they could yield wool that might compete with the wool from England. The New York Society for the Promotion of Arts, Agriculture and Economy introduced, among other things, the manufacture of linen, and similar organizations in Philadelphia introduced the culture of flax. Great movements of this sort would be doomed to futility unless the women co-operated, and in this case they did so, nobly. They consented to see their husbands and lovers in homespun rather than English cloth. They got out and dusted off and oiled and put back into operation old, all but forgotten spinning wheels, and with these, massed in churches or other meeting houses, they held day-long sessions of spinning and gossip. Some of them even swore off tea, for the duration. The high-minded unmarried women of Providence and Bristol, Rhode Island, solemnly vowed that they would not accept the advances of any man who was opposed to repeal of the Stamp Act. Sacrifices like these bring folks together.

Money, such as there was of it, crept out of hiding. Despite the presence of so much of the British Navy—and its dependence upon impressment—and despite a drastic cut in the molasses tariff, good times appeared reluctant to come back. Smuggling, the sign of a pinch, was on the increase.[31] The new infant industries sagged or faded away entirely. Not many men in America seemed to have faith in the future. On the surface of it they might have been thought back where they had long wished to be—in the flourishing condition they knew in the days of Burke's "salutory neglect," the days before the end of the French and Indian War, before 1763 and all this pesky mercantilism. Actually, they weren't; and most of them knew or sensed this.

They could not believe that England would take such a defeat lying down. And they were right.

CHAPTER

11

ENGLISHMEN DON'T VOTE

SAMUEL JOHNSON (who knew everything) knew about Americans. "They are a race of convicts," he pronounced, "and ought to be thankful for anything we allow them short of hanging."

There were many at Home who agreed.

When a person every whit as pontifical as Dr. Johnson, and in station so much more august, namely Lord Mansfield, chief justice of the King's Bench, proclaimed publicly, before the assembled peers, that "virtual representation" was the logical, legal, and indeed inevitable system for the British Empire, then what Englishman could doubt that this was so? Milord wore his robes while he said it, too.

"Virtual representation" was not a new thing. It was a theory, frequently advanced by the privileged few, that every member of the House of Commons represented every district and every class in the Empire, not simply his own home constituents. In other words, each squire whose primary interests were fox-hunting and the reduction of taxes, and whether or not he attended the sessions of Parliament, represented, equally, impartially, the Carolina rice planters, the Virginia tobacco planters, the New York fur dealers, and the Connecticut distillers of rum, presumably understanding all the problems of all these persons.

Some manner of justification had to be set up for the system of apportioning Commons seats, which stank. Though the principle of no taxation without representation could be traced back to the Magna Carta and had been clearly restated in the Bill of Rights of 1689, there was not, in the Commons, even a token gesture toward anything like distributed representation. In the first place, only one out of every thirty adult male Englishmen was entitled to vote. Out of a population of about 8,000,000 there were some 160,000 who elected the members of the Commons.

Some seats were pieces of personal property, like books, like paintings, or snuffboxes. The Duke of Norfolk had eleven such in his pocket; Lord Lonsdale had nine, Lord Darlington seven, and so it went.

Old Sarum, population nothing, had two members of the Commons. The shires of Cornwall and Devon had seventy between them, while London, Westminster, and Southwark, all together, had only six, and the flourishing cities of Manchester, Birmingham, and Sheffield had none at all.

What American would wish, even if he were able, to be thrust into any such crazy-quilt conference? What would it mean if he was? How much would his vote count?

Yet there were those, on both sides of the sea, who believed, or who *had* believed, that colonial representation in the Commons was the only answer to the problem that loomed so large these days.

What the King thought of this, if he thought of it at all, we do not know; but it is mentionable that not a single Whig leader, even among those who were friends of the American colonies—Camden, Conway, Burke, Pitt—favored any such plan.

The Atlantic made up the biggest barrier. The trip ordinarily occupied two months, each way; so that any colonial M.P. who aspired to keep in touch with his constituents at least once a year—and the colonists would not want any other kind—would spend much of his time tossing in a ship. Additionally, the time such a person did spend in London would be largely wasted, since the great majority of the matters debated and passed upon by the Commons related to purely British matters, having nothing to do with America.

To send such delegates, even if it were legally convenient, would be against the natural law, said Americans, so many of whom in those days loved to talk about the natural law. Still, there were idealists; there were hopers.

The Stamp Act and the events leading to it and away from it changed much of this. Joseph Galloway in Philadelphia continued to urge an imperial federation, but James Otis of Boston recanted his original stand, for he had been disillusioned, and the same thing applied to Benjamin Franklin in London, where he had come to know the full rottenness of British politics.

Thomas Crowley, an English Quaker, a merchant who had traveled widely in America, and Francis Maseres, a member of the Inner Temple, formerly attorney general of Quebec, had advanced and continued to push plans for an imperial federation, an evenness of all partners in the Empire; but they did not get far; and Adam Smith, who was strong for such a plan, was one whose voice at this time was not loud in the land.[32]

On a lower level there were many M.P.s who were shocked at the thought of an influx of "pumpkin senators" into the House of Commons, which, after all, was a gentlemen's club, so to speak. Would you, sir, care to sit in the same chamber with such barbarians, smelling, doubtless, of the pig sty? And in a little while—the damned colonies were growing so fast—they would monopolize the house. And their very presence would inspire some of our own undesirable backcountry boors to ask why *they* should not be admitted as well. It was a disquieting reflection.

Quite as shocked by this proposal were the colonists, by and large. What! send some of our finest sons to that den of iniquity? Rather send them directly to Hell! Toss them into the pit Abaddon guards! Doom them to everlasting disgrace!

Apart from the obvious difficulties of deciding how many members of Parliament should be sent and from which colonies, there were moral objections. Everybody knew what life was like in London, with its balls and pleasure gardens and its —well, bagnios. American M.P.s, newly arrived, might be, probably would be, Godfearing men; but they would be dizzied, they would be bewildered and led astray, and sooner or later they would sell their votes and sink down and down. . . . No, a thousand times no! The system of employing unofficial colonial agents by the year might have its faults, might be a makeshift,[33] but it was better, anything would be better, than exposing pure, decent, upright Americans to the dangers and deceits, the pitfalls and perils, of London politics.

12

TO BISHOP OR NOT TO BISHOP

IT WAS REPORTED that in eighteenth-century Massachusetts the sight of a pair of lawn sleeves would cause more con-
sternation than the sight of a thousand Mohawks in full war
paint; for bishops meant slavery. The same might have been
said of almost any of the other colonies, even Virginia, where
the Church of England was more or less officially ensconced.
This was proved by the unprecedented wave of hard feeling
caused by another flareup of the no-bishops-here debate at this
touchy time.[34]

Nobody knows how the mainland American colonies
happened to get under the see of the Bishop of London in the
first place, unless it was because in 1620 the Virginia Company
asked the current bishop (who was a stockholder) to let them
have a few clerics for their struggling new little settlement at
Jamestown—something, incidentally, the bishop did not do.
Anyway, there it was. Most bishops of London seemed rather
eager to get rid of the colonies, though they did not know how;
but there were exceptions. None ever visited them, nor did
any other bishop.

The Church of England was distinctly a national institution. It had been designed as such. A certain amount of it, to be sure, naturally oozed over into Scotland and Ireland, but no arrangements ever had been made, or even contemplated, for it to cross the sea. It simply was not equipped for such a voyage.

The Roman Catholic Church was different; its discipline was well fixed, its aims stabilized; and the wild lands of the New World did not faze it. France had done little enough about Canada, which after all was a frozen wasteland, but Spain was lavish with bishops and even archbishops in Latin America.[35]

A bishop of the Church of England was a peer of the realm, with a seat in the House of Lords. Such a personage lived in a palace and was attended by a large entourage. To keep up his dignity, to discharge even the simplest of his functions, he needed an income of at least £1,000 a year. Who would pay? The early colonists were poor; nor were they notably fond of peers in any form.

Yet if the Church was to spread in America, as was hoped, some sort of official fatherly hand was needed. Who would confirm? who would ordain? Suffragans were never sent, it is hard to see why. Commissaries were sent instead, but they were never satisfactory, for they were unsure of their own authority and the local priests were leery of them. Commissaries could confirm, but they could not ordain. Anybody in America who aspired to enter the ranks of the Anglican clergy had to make the long, arduous, costly trip to the mother country, there to get himself ordained by a real bishop, and then he faced the costly, arduous, and long journey back before he could practice his new profession. There were not many colonists dedicated enough, and rich enough, to do that.

Much depended upon the attitude of the monarch, who

was titular head of the Church of England. James I was not troubled by American colonial problems, for the colonies amounted to very little in his time, but his son and successor, Charles I, a profoundly religious man, was; and so was Charles's chief theological advisor, Archbishop Laud, who strongly favored a foreign bishopric. However, Laud was charged with Popery, and his head was chopped off, and King Charles's head too was chopped off, and at the end of the Civil War and during the years of the Protectorate the Church of England had all it could do just to stay alive, much less spread itself. Came the Restoration, and Charles II, the Merry Monarch, proved to be much more interested in mistresses than in missionaries. Charles was a deathbed convert to Rome, and might well have been a Catholic in his heart all the time. His brother and successor, James II, was an out-and-out Catholic, which fact cost him his throne. William of Orange, William III, was called the Protestant Champion, as indeed he was, but his was a political mind, and he understood little of the church he headed and probably cared less; and the same might be said of his wife and co-monarch, that cipher, Mary. When Mary's pudgy sister climbed to the throne, however, it was another story. Anne may not have been bright, but devout she certainly was. Those who believed in an American bishopric took heart.

There had always been some of them, and now they came out into the open. As early as 1685 Sir Leoline Jenkyns in his will left enough to establish two fellowships in Jesus College, Oxford, with the stipulation that the money was to be used for the first American bishopric, if ever one was established. In 1715 Archbishop Tenison left £1,000 for such a bishopric, and pending its foundation the money should be used as a pension for the oldest missionary in the colonial service. Dugald Campbell in 1720 and Lady Elizabeth Hastings in 1741 each left £500 for this purpose. Paul Fisher of Clifton, near Bristol, in 1763 left £1,000 "for the use of the first bishop that shall be appointed in America," and soon afterward the Bishop of London himself left £500 for attainment of the same end.[36]

The Society for Propagating the Gospel in Foreign Parts, a Church of England child, was established in London in 1701, the year before Anne's accession, and it was soon to get her full blessing as queen.

The Society set up many Episcopal churches in America, and, when called upon, it supported them from privately raised funds. This still was not a bishop, though from the beginning the Society was strongly in favor of the establishment of a bishopric in America. Its enemies on the continent—and they were many, and they were virulent—accused the Society of being much more interested in getting a bishop and all of the glitter that goes with one than in the spiritual welfare of the Indians, much less that of the Negro slaves, the masters of whom, perhaps on the assumption that they had none, showed scant concern with their souls.

Its very name was against the Society, not because it was cumbersome but because it sounded condescending. Most of the American colonies, and certainly the "saints" of New England, descendants of the original pilgrims and Puritans, felt no need to have the Gospel propagated in their midst. They knew their Bible up and down, backwards and forwards, without the aid of any bishop. They had been brought up on it. They could quote any part of it at a moment's notice, and frequently did.

Fourteen Church of England clergymen, assembled informally at Burlington, New Jersey, in 1705, sent a petition Home asking for the consecration of a Bishop of New Jersey. They had already bought a residence for him, on their own.[37]

Real preparations went into this petition, and real plans were to come out of it. Jonathan Swift, dean of St. Patrick's, Dublin, who had always wanted to be a bishop, thought highly enough of the possibility to start assembling his political armament with the aim of getting the post for himself; but when he learned that it was not to be a sinecure, that he would actually be expected to *go* there, he backed out. Even so, there were many other potential candidates; and the thing might have gone through if it had not been for the death of Queen Anne.

Of each of her two long-lived successors, the first Georges, it might be said, as it has been said of so many monarchs, *"Cuius regio eius religio,"* or, "Where he resides, that's his religion." They were Protestants all right, but neither could be described as an ardent Anglican; and the American bishopric plan lagged from lack of interest in high places.

When George III came to the throne the bishop-wishers' hopes rose yet again, for *this* Defender of the Faith was a zealous Church of England man.

Meanwhile, Episcopalians in America, stepchildren, got along as best they could. There were churches in all of the colonies, but most of them were dependent upon the SPG, as its members liked to call it, and were concentrated in the cities, having little real touch with the people by and large.

Returning SPG missionaries invariably bemoaned the lack of an American bishop. The Americans of whatever faith, they would say, were ready for Anglicanism. A certain amount of snobbery entered into this. The royal governors were, most of them, members of the Church of England; and it was around them, in their respective little "courts," that whatever social life the various colonies knew was centered. The Church of England, in other words, was the fashionable church. It would be even more so, the returning missionaries avowed, if there were a bishop on the spot. Yet it was for this very reason that the royal governors refused to promote the cause. With a bishop on the premises not only would a governor's own luster be somewhat dimmed but a certain amount of his power —not much, to be sure, but every little bit counted—would be taken from him.

Virginia and Maryland were the only colonies in which the Church of England was truly installed, yet in Maryland and Virginia too there was stiff opposition to the plan for an American bishop. This could well be because of the priests assigned to the colonial benefices. In the other colonies the Anglican ministers were either SPGs, men wedded to their work, or else they were priests who had gone all the way to England to *become* priests, in itself a testimonial of their devotion. In Virginia and Maryland they could be and too often were the sort of young priests who had not worked out well at Home, the clergymen the Church wished to be rid of without disgrace—drunks, debtors, misfits, nitwits—in accordance with the English remittance-man tradition. A bishop might have done much to keep such clerics in line, but the Marylanders and Virginians, discouraged by what they saw, did not care to chance it.

North and South, and in the middle colonies as well, as feeling got higher and hotter, as war neared, it was remarked by many that the Anglican clergy were not only conservative but stubbornly loyal. For every exception like John Peter Gabriel Muhlenberg [38] there were scores of priests who undeviatingly supported the King and his ministers. These included some of the most distinguished clergymen in the colonies, such as Samuel Seabury of Connecticut, Dr. Samuel Auchmuty of Trinity Church, New York, Dr. Charles Inglis, who was to become the first Bishop of Nova Scotia, President Myles Cooper of King's College (later Columbia), and Thomas Bradbury Chandler of St. John's Church, Elizabethtown, New Jersey.

These clerics and certain others like them used to meet once a year to talk over their position. It was entirely unofficial; it was unauthorized, informal, but the nearest thing to a bishops' convocation that America was allowed. In 1767, the year after the repeal of the Stamp Act, these men persuaded one of their number, Dr. Chandler, to publish a pamphlet, "Appeal to the Public in Behalf of the Church of England in America," expressing the opinions of them all in favor of an American bishop—a bishop who would have no secular powers.

This, a reasoned, mild, firmly non-political treatise, brought about a deafening detonation. Much to his own astonishment, Dr. Chandler was answered from all directions, but most vehemently from New England, where a mere mention of bishops might bring about a brawl. Nor were these answers soft, calculated to turn away wrath. They were furious. They sizzled.

"Will they never let us rest in peace—except where all the weary are at rest?" raged Jonathan Mayhew, an eminent Boston Congregationalist. "Is it not enough that they persecuted us out of the Old World? Will they pursue us into the New?—to convert us here, compassing sea and land to make us proselytes, while they neglect the heathen and heathenish plantations? What other New World remains as a sanctuary for us from their oppressions, in case of need? Where is the Columbus to explore one for us, and pilot us to it, before we are consumed by the flames, or deluged in a flood, of Episcopacy?" [39]

This and much more like it went on for several years, resulting, in the end, only in a great deal of hard feeling on both sides.

In fact, the bishopric-for-America pleas probably never had a chance, there being formidable opposition to it at Home.

This opposition came from three classes: (1) Whigs, who did not want any increase in the House of Lords, bishops being almost all of them Tories; (2) dissenters, who did not want the episcopal establishment to spread anywhere anyhow; and (3) clerics, who disliked the talk of a bishop without secular powers, which might lead to almost anything.[40]

CHAPTER

13

WINE AND A WEATHERCOCK

THE SPOILED CHILD of the House of Commons was called "Champagne Charlie" in part because one of his wittiest speeches—a speech made while he was drunk, as so many of his best speeches were—pertained to that wine; but in part too, because Charles Townshend was effervescent, he was volatile, he was heady, he glittered and fizzed. They also called him the Weathercock, which amused him. Consistency, he thought, was for the dull. Himself, he could change his policy as quickly as he changed his waistcoat, and both would be bright. A younger son who had married well, this sprig of the nobility must have been the most asked-out man in London.

He had spurned a spot in the Rockingham cabinet, which after struggling along for a year, all the while striving to get the great Pitt to join up, in the summer of 1766 at last came apart at the seams. Then and only then did Mr. Pitt consent to take command, and Champagne Charlie, to the astonishment of almost everybody, probably including himself, was made chancellor of the exchequer.

It was a skittery assignment, the finances of the nation being what they were, and the situation in the American colonies being what *it* was, but even though he first had to give up the much more lucrative job of paymaster general he accepted blithely.

Landowners were paying four shillings to the pound on their land, and they moaned. Townshend sympathized with them. Airily he said that he hoped soon to have this reduced to three shillings; whereupon his predecessor, William Dowdeswell, took him at his word and caused Parliament to pass just such a cut. This made an enormous hole in the treasury.

Pitt was furious. He thought of demanding Townshend's resignation. But he was himself teetering on the brink of uncertainty, for once in his life not sure of himself. Unexpectedly, and before he consented to become the King's first minister, he insisted that he be created a nobleman.

No sooner said than done. He became, in a wink, the Earl of Chatham. A man prodigiously vain, he was pricked to the quick when he learned that his public, by and large, did not look with approval upon the sight of the Great Commoner becoming a Lord. It was bad enough in England, as his sensitive ear told him, but it was even worse in the American colonies, where until this time he had been idolized as the man who had whipped the Stamp Act: many statues had been erected to him, one, white marble, in Wall Street, New York, representing him in a Roman toga.

This response dismayed and bewildered Pitt. He hesitated over the Townshend matter; and as he hesitated he came down with—well, something—some black ailment. Nobody knew what really possessed the colossus. A form of insanity, perhaps? He was in pain, but it was not just gout. He went to Bath, but he did not take the waters, only sat groaning in a darkened room, refusing to see anybody for more than a few minutes at a time, refusing even to discuss politics. He complained that his eyes hurt him. His speech did not make sense.

But *somebody* had to run the government, and the Honorable Charles Townshend cheerfully volunteered. There was nobody to stop him, and the newly created earl, burbling at Bath, did not know what was going on. Always excepting Pitt himself, Charles Townshend was the best orator and the sharpest Parliamentarian in the cabinet, which he readily controlled. Half a million missing out of the revenue, because of the reduction of the land tax? He would make it up. He had a plan in mind, he said. He intimated that it would involve getting the money, or part of the money anyway, from the American colonies.

Here was why they called him the Weathercock. He always showed the way the wind was blowing. There were against-America mutters all over the House, even among the squires, only partially mollified by the land-tax cut. Maybe it had been a bad idea, after all, to repeal that Stamp Tax? There were the colonists, every one of them rich, fat, and paying no taxes at all, squealing like pigs, indeed, if anybody even *mentioned* taxes to them. Why shouldn't they be made to disgorge at least a part of their share of keeping up the Empire?

Townshend smelled this attitude, and played up to it. Ignoring for the moment that whipping-boy, that most annoying and most impertinent city, Boston, he proposed to the House of Commons that the New York Assembly's powers be suspended until such time as the colony was willing to abide by the Mutiny Act of 1763.

The Mutiny Act, so far as it concerned the colonies, had nothing to do with mutiny. One provision stipulated that any colony in which royal troops were posted must supply those troops with living quarters (unless there were publicly owned buildings available), fuel, candles, vinegar, salt, and either beer or cider. This had seemed harmless enough, before the repeal of the Stamp Act; but the colonists were waxing increasingly touchy to anything that smacked of taxation, and now they began to ask themselves—or the ones in New York did anyway, New York being the headquarters of the British Army in America—if this provision was not, after all, just another hidden tax. Abruptly the New York Assembly refused to supply the vinegar, the salt, the beer. It did supply the rest.

It was not the cost of these articles that caused the Assembly to bridle. It was the principle of the thing. The Assembly wished it to be understood that this was a gift, not a weak answer to a demand.

Whatever it was, Parliament, at Charles Townshend's motion, picked up the gauntlet. Townshend was opposed to the sending over of eight or ten regiments of the line, as many members proposed. That would only serve to unite the colonies. But he did persuade the Commons to suspend the New York Assembly.

Those would have been fighting words at any other time, and might have caused all manner of resentment in the colonies, not just New York either, but for the fact that the Assembly, having asserted itself, having blown off steam, having, as it supposed, made its point, already had retracted its refusal to supply the beer, vinegar, salt. It had not done this through fear. The Parliamentary "freeze" was voted July 2, 1767, but the Assembly, on May 26, before it had heard of any threat, already had retracted. Both sides, as a result, were left looking a little foolish. And Champagne Charlie had to seek another issue.

He was ready for this. Until now he had not been known as either pro- or anti-colonies—he had voted for the Stamp

Act but he had also voted for its repeal—but now he proposed new duties, out-and-out, unmistakable duties, on five varieties of glass, white and red lead, painters' colors, tea, and sixty-seven grades of paper.

He was sure that there would be no objections to these duties on the part of the Americans. How could there be, when the Americans themselves had said that they did not object to external, only to internal taxes? So this was what they wanted. So he was giving it to them. "Perfect nonsense" was the way he described the internal-external distinction to the Commons; but if the Americans liked it that way, why not keep them happy? [41]

The brightest ornament in Pitt's "Mosaic Ministry"—so called because it contained so many seemingly conflicting members, it being Pitt's idea, as it was the King's, that no one party should run the government—somewhat dampened the spirits of the members of Commons when he predicted that the proposed duties would raise only about £40,000 a year. This was a mere drop in the bucket; but Townshend hastened to point out that, as the New York Assembly had believed, it was the *principle* of the thing that counted: once Parliament's right to collect from the colonies had been established, there was no telling where it might stop. Seemingly it did not occur to the Honorable Charles Townshend that the colonists might think the same thing.

There were a few hardheads who mumbled that this legislation could cause a renewal of the trouble, but Charles Townshend was supremely confident, and the act passed, quietly enough, 180 to 98.

It was to go into effect November 20, 1767. Champagne Charlie died, somewhat unexpectedly, September 4 of that year. He was pleased with his accomplishment, right to the end. Hadn't he solved the whole problem? Wasn't he a bright boy?

14

A FRESH FOOL

THE PREAMBLE of the Townshend Acts provided that
funds raised under these acts were to be used for "defraying
the Charge of the Administration of Justice, and the Support
of Civil Government, in such Provinces where it shall be
found necessary; and toward further defraying the Expenses
of defending, protecting, and securing the said Dominions."

Here was a note that sounded ominous to the Americans.
Not only was Parliament about to tax them but it planned to
use this tax to pay the troops it might quarter upon them and,
even worse, to pay the salaries of the royal governors, lieutenant governors, judges, and the like. It was as though the
colonies were being made to finance their own castration. On
the same day that the Townshend Acts were passed there was
passed also a bill providing for the establishment of an American Board of Customs Commissioners, with jurisdiction over
the entire coast north of the Florida Straits and including Ber-
muda, the Bahamas, and Nova Scotia. The headquarters of
this board was to be—Boston. Moreover, plans were under
way to establish three more vice-admiralty courts—at Boston,
Philadelphia, and Charleston.

All of this would make smuggling much more difficult, even dangerous; yet how were the colonists to live without smuggling?

And what about the goods already smuggled into the colonies but not yet distributed? Almost every merchant had a warehouse bulging with contraband, which now he would have to sell as soon as possible, perhaps at ruinous prices, since the new law, which had real teeth in it, specifically authorized the issuance of writs of assistance.

Clearly the new administration meant business, a circumstance the more dismaying to the American merchants because they had only recently been so cheered by the repeal of the Stamp Act followed by a return to the premiership of their great good friend William Pitt.

The new arrivals, the men who were to enforce these carefully thought-out laws, were a rugged lot, a grim lot.[42] The old customs agents, with whom the merchants had got along so well for so many years, with whom they had enjoyed such convenient "understandings," were summarily dismissed from their jobs, and the tight-lipped newcomers appeared prepared to—of all things!—live on their salaries.

Those salaries, it was no comfort to remember, were to come out of the duties paid perforce by the American merchants.

Governor Bernard of Massachusetts, a timorous man, who was easily panicked, again and again had written to London that the town of Boston was the villain of this whole piece, that all sedition originated and festered there. Bernard wailed that his very life was in danger in Boston, and that the only place he was safe was within the walls of Fort William, behind which from time to time, frightened, he took refuge. Hutchinson too, the lieutenant governor, though a much stauncher soul, a person who would scorn to seek the shelter of Fort William, habitually in his reports decried the "levelling" behavior of the Bostonians—the backcountry residents of Massachusetts were all right—and stated that in his opinion the radical Whigs were out for nothing less than complete independence. Certainly Boston, as it was the nearest American city to Home, was the noisiest of them, the most troublesome. The sack of Hutchinson's house had not been forgotten. The mobs in New York were bad enough; the mobs in Boston were intolerable.

Bostonians, not entirely without reason, thought that the Townshend Acts were largely aimed at them, that Whitehall strove to make an example of Boston. Customs men there, Navy men too, were at their nastiest.

Boston took up the challenge, if challenge it was, and originated the second wave of non-importation agreements. Soon all up and down the land the spinning wheels could be heard again. The students at Harvard swore off tea, and the graduating class wore homespun gowns. The students at Yale swore off foreign liquor. The South Carolina Assemblymen wore caps instead of the previously obligatory, made-in-England wigs. Lamb disappeared from the butcher shops. Elaborate mourning methods once again were scowled upon. Christopher Gadsden went to his wife's funeral in a suit of blue homespun. Where there had been about three hundred ships a year between America and England before the Townshend Acts, there were now fewer than one hundred, and not all of those were fully loaded.

Boston went further. The Massachusetts General Court (Assembly) under the direct influence of the "Boston seat," February 11, 1768, issued a Circular Letter denouncing the Townshend Acts.

Sam Adams, as clerk of the house, wrote the Circular Letter, but the one that went out surely was not his own first draft. It was altogether too mild in tone. Yet it was firm! Directed to the houses of representatives of the other colonies, it urged them to petition for the repeal of the Townshend Acts as being a violation of the colonists' constitutional rights as Englishmen. No taxation without representation was its quiet but insistent cry. It brushed aside as not worth discussion the theory of "virtual" representation, and said that actual representation would not have been desirable even if it had been possible. It made no dire threats. It even protested, once again, the loyalty of the colonies, and decried any thought of independence from the mother country.

Governor Bernard was in a dither about it; but then, he was always in a dither about something. Outside, in the various assemblies to which it was sent, the Circular Letter caused little stir. A few endorsed it, but without enthusiasm. Many ignored it. Quaker-dominated Pennsylvania received and examined it with misgiving. Without the endorsement of Pennsylvania, that keystone state astraddle of the north-south route, the thing would have fallen flat; and Pennsylvania was on the verge of passing it by—when a fresh fool appeared upon the stage.

Lord Hillsborough was occupying—he was the first occupant of—a new office: secretary of state for the colonies. His earldom was Irish, but the man himself was English to the core. That he knew nothing about the colonies he was secretary of state for was revealed in his behavior on this occasion.

Rather than of William Pitt, the colonists should have raised statues of such founders of American liberty as George Grenville, Champagne Charlie Townshend—and Lord Hillsborough.

All agog, Hillsborough hurried to the King, and George III gave him permission to write a sharp Circular Letter of his own, which he promptly did. Colonial governors—excepting those of Connecticut and Rhode Island whom even Hillsborough did not presume to dictate to—were to forbid their popular houses of legislation to endorse the Massachusetts Circular Letter, "which will be treating it with the contempt it deserves," and if any should be so ill-advised as to do so anyway the governor should immediately prorogue it. As for Massachusetts Assembly, it must immediately rescind "that rash and hasty proceeding," for until it did so it stood suspended, its authority gone.

In other words, a titled dimwit of whom most Americans had never even heard at a stroke of his pen was depriving them of rights they had enjoyed for more than a hundred and fifty years. The Declaratory Act might have been a mere face-saving device. The suspension of the New York Assembly had caused some disquietude in the colonies, though the circumstances that surrounded it were such that it had no effect. But—*this!* The veriest American Tory would have to splutter about this.

James Otis hooted that the damned thing wasn't even well written. "Any schoolboy," he averred, could have done a better job.

Pennsylvania immediately endorsed the Massachusetts Circular Letter, and so did virtually every other colony, most of them with expression of approval that went almost as far as Sam Adams would have gone if left to himself.

Somebody in the Massachusetts General Court had the temerity to move that the Circular Letter be rescinded. The vote against this was 92 to 17. The ninety-two were hailed as heroes. Paul Revere, that sturdy middle-aged horseman, designed and executed a silver punch bowl honoring their number and their vote. The seventeen saw themselves listed in the *Gazette* as enemies of their country. Friends refused to speak to them on the street. Revere drew a cartoon showing them descending into Hell, an act that made even the Devil wince. Their retirement from public life was certain. Sam Adams went so far (without a shred of evidence) as to label them Roman Catholics; and no man could live *that* down.

15

THE TROUBLES OF A

MERCURIAL MAN

JOHN HANCOCK was a mercurial man, personally unpredictable. There were times when the Whigs were sure that they had him securely in their camp; but there were other times when the Tories almost thought that they had lured him over to *their* side, where, being rich, he belonged. It might have been the Townshend Acts, as much as anything else, that finally determined him to stick with his first love, the radicals.

John Hancock now was the hero, once more, of the South Enders and North Enders alike, for not only were they awed by his wealth and flattered by the fact that he sought them out, but they liked his habit of producing a pipe of wine on the occasion of any impromptu celebration: he was a quick man with a bung.

Wine from the Azores was an exceedingly important part of the New England economy, particularly desirable because it was paid for with produce rather than with hard money, which was so scarce in the colonies. This trade could not continue to flourish, however, if duty was paid on the wine, as the government in England demanded.

Hancock's fast sloop *Liberty* was reputed to be loaded with wine from Madeira when it put into Boston on a day in May of '68. It was made fast, and the boys prepared to unload it. Then a tidesman came aboard. The *Liberty* could not be unloaded, he said, until it had cleared customs.

Now, what was this? What sort of way was this to treat a vessel that belonged to John Hancock? The offending official, an obscure part-time employee of the customs house named Thomas Kirk, was ushered belowdecks and locked there. For three hours he heard a great tramping and bumping and the squeal of cranes. Then he was released—and the ship was empty. Hancock had a lot of friends.

This, at any rate, was the Crown's story when, a whole month later, on a purely technical charge, the customs commissioners seized the *Liberty*, by that time loaded with 200 barrels of whale oil and 20 barrels of tar earmarked for England. The cargo was seized along with the vessel, and Hancock and five other Boston merchants were arrested on a charge of having smuggled in 100 pipes of wine, valued at £30 a pipe, after failing to pay £700 in duties. Each was sued by the Crown for £9,000, a total of £54,000.

Hancock denied the charge. He said that the *Liberty* had carried only 25 *casks* of wine (a cask was a small barrel; but a pipe was the equivalent of half a tun—that is, four full barrels) for himself and a few friends, and·that these had been declared and the duty paid. The Crown's case rested on Thomas Kirk's unsupported story, and Kirk stood to make more than he could have made in twenty years of honest toil; for the law gave one third of the seizure to the informer, one third to the governor, one third to the Crown. Yet though Kirk's story could not be supported, neither could it be refuted, for between the time when the *Liberty* entered Boston harbor and the time, a month later, when she was seized, the captain had died, and the crew had been scattered.

The case, which had political roots far away in London, dragged on—in vice-admiralty court—for months; and at last it was dismissed.

Meanwhile, Boston had another riot on its hands. Unlike some of the previous ones, this was spontaneous. The sight of the *Liberty* being towed under the guns of the warship *Romney* in a frameup so patently aimed to "get" the patriot Hancock, was too much for the crowd. Nobody urged them on, nobody harangued them. In a body they hurried to the homes of the comptroller, the collector, the customs inspector.

They had threatened these men in the past, as they had threatened the hated commissioners. On March 4, and again on March 18, the anniversary of the Stamp Act repeal, they had demonstrated in strength before the commissioners' houses; but no stone had been hurled. The situation was especially tense because the refusal of the Boston carpenters to accept two shillings three pence a day instead of the three shillings they demanded had resulted in many of the shipyards moving to nearby towns where labor was less expensive, and Boston itself was crowded with the traditionally tinderlike unemployed.

The inspector, the collector, and the comptroller were mauled, not too badly. They took the inspector's sword and broke it. They hauled his boat up on the Common and burned it. They smashed the windows of all three of their houses. Then they went looking for the commissioners—but the commissioners already were on their way to the *Romney*, a fifty-gun ship that had earlier been sent in answer to their pleas for protection.

It was not much of a mob, as mobs went, and the very haphazardousness of it argued again that it had no leader: if Mackintosh had been there, or Sam Swift, the North End gang leader, there would have been a more bitter story.

The fact remained, however, that the King's servants had been set upon and beaten, the King's commissioners for fear of their lives forced to take refuge in a warship. This, clearly, could not be tolerated. Lord Hillsborough, secretary of state for the colonies, wrote to General Gage in New York ordering him to send two regiments to Boston to keep order.[43] Gage had them ready. He had for some time been expecting this order. Indeed, after the August, 1765, riots, the Stamp Act riots, Gage had written to Governor Bernard offering him the use of one hundred troopers, but Bernard at that time thought that a mere hundred would only cause additional trouble.

Samuel Adams, that master thimblerigger, the "Incendiary-in-Chief," as Hutchinson called him, had developed his town meeting technique to the point of perfection. Together with James Otis he could cause a town meeting to be called at any time, and once it was assembled it would eat out of his hand.

When the General Court of Massachusetts refused to rescind the Circular Letter, Governor Bernard, in accordance with his orders from Lord Hillsborough, dissolved that body for the rest of the year. He acted just in time. They had been about to adopt a resolution demanding his recall. Their contention was that he grossly misrepresented them to Whitehall; and it was to be admitted that his reports, as well as his letters to friends in England, were filled with the blackest foreboding, for the man seemed really to believe that he was living in a cauldron of rebelliousness.

Otis and Adams and Cushing, the speaker, then called a town meeting. Governor Bernard did not like these town meetings, which he regarded as democracy on a rampage— and illegal to boot.

Massachusetts had a comparatively low property qualification for voting, £40, and there might have been 700 to 800 adult males in Boston who could meet this. Nevertheless, Bernard complained, at town meetings attended by at least that many men everybody voted, nobody was examined as to his qualification. (Later, when excitement had mounted, the Caucus Club devised another type of mass meeting, called "meetings of the body," to which were invited the residents of all nearby towns; and once again anybody could vote. These were not, properly, town meetings, though they had much the same effect.)

This particular meeting petitioned the Governor to reconvene the General Court, a gesture. He didn't do so, of course. He couldn't—his orders being what they were.

Another town meeting was promptly called, and this one ordered the Selectmen to issue a call for a "committee of convention." This had an ominous sound; and it was made even more ominous when the same town meeting recommended that every male citizen of Boston supply himself with "a well fixed Firelock Musket, accoutrement, and ammunition" because of the danger of a war with France, which was preposterous. Then the meeting named, as the Boston delegates to this "committee of convention," Otis, Adams, Cushing, and Hancock, the regular occupants of the "Boston seat" in the legislature.

That was the plan: to make it look as much like the legislature as possible. It could not *be* the legislature, for that body, according to the very charter that the Whigs were so fond of quoting, could only be called into being by the Governor; but it could *look* like it.

During the summer the General Court had seldom functioned anyway, but with the approach of fall the Caucus Club boys missed it, and besides they wished to sound out colony-wide sentiment on how to greet the soon-to-appear troops. Sam Adams at least really seemed to think that this informal assemblage might yet be turned into a revolutionary body and that thousands of armed patriots could be called in to resist the landing. He went around babbling this.

Rumors flew. On the London Exchange stocks fell. There was, indisputably, a war scare. Would the colonists resist?

The convention sat September 22, and there were present seventy delegates from sixty-four towns and districts. To keep up the resemblance to the dissolved body this unauthorized convention nominated Thomas Cushing, the General Court speaker, as chairman.

The convention, an uneasy one, lasted a week; and by the end of that time it was attended by delegates from ninety-six town and districts, which was about as fair a showing as the General Court itself ordinarily had made—and indeed, the great majority of the delegates *had been* members of the General Court.

There were no fireworks. Adams and the other Boston Sons of Liberty worked furiously "out of doors"—that is, in the lobby—but they could not egg the countrymen into violence. On the floor itself the proceedings were downright tame. There were adopted two petitions to the Governor, a letter to the General Court's agent in London, De Berdt, and a set of fairly meek resolutions. That was all.

On the day that they adjourned *sine die* word was brought that the first of the troopships was off Nantucket. Two days later the soldiers came ashore at Boston.

Nothing happened.

CHAPTER

16

THE UNSPEAKABLES

GREAT BRITAIN'S CABINET went on playing its game of musical chairs, but it wobbled—undeniably it wobbled. General Conway had dropped out. Hillsborough, somewhat subdued now, continued to be secretary of state for the colonies. Pitt's place had been taken, tenuously, by the tall, dark, and somewhat sinister-seeming Duke of Grafton; but the upcoming leader, a King's Man, was Lord North.

There was nothing sinister about North. If he played the Parliamentary game the way he found it, he played it jovially and well. He was faithful to his monarch, and could keep the members in line, delivering the goods, judiciously distributing favors. A great schemer, he didn't look the part, being plump, pale, and pop-eyed, with a receding chin and a receding forehead: in truth, he looked and acted a great deal like an intelligent George III, though there is no reason to believe that the two really were related. North could not make much of a speech, but he knew how to get along with politicians. He was a great worker "out of doors." In the Commons itself, during debate, he had a tendency to doze; but there was nothing wrong in that.

105

In the early days of his second ministry, Pitt, when he was shocked by the reckless behavior of Townshend, had gone to North in the hope of persuading him to take over the chancellery of the exchequer; but North didn't like the setup; he wanted something safer. It was generally predicted that he would be the next prime minister.

The non-importation campaign was not going well. True, the English merchants must have been feeling the pinch: Pennsylvania, for instance, had been late to come in, some time after New England and New York, yet, when once she did, her imports from Great Britain fell sharply—£441,829 in 1768, £204,978 in 1769, £134,881 in 1770. But the South, which had a system of factors, usually English or Scottish, rather than local merchants, was not much interested; and the American merchants themselves, in the middle and northern states, were not as keenly concerned as they had been at the time of the Stamp Tax, for after all they had only to pass the extra price on to the wholesalers, who in their turn passed it to the retailer, who passed it to the ultimate consumer. Often enough it was necessary to call in the Liberty Boys in order that a maverick might be made to see the light.

Committees of correspondence were formed, and these helped somewhat, but there still was no central inspiration, and in the ordinary course of events the loose understanding— it was no more than that—would surely fall apart. There was some faint talk of another congress, but the failure of the Massachusetts "committee of convention" did not encourage it.

Part of the campaign was devoted to encouraging the manufacture of home products previously bought from England,[44] but these were for the most part unexciting products— starch, glue, hair powder, snuff—and, as before, the men with the money were leery of investing, fearful as they were that the whole business would soon blow over. Americans still insisted that they were not a nation of manufacturers but rather a nation of seamen, shipbuilders, and farmers.

As for the war between the shipping men and 'the new, tough customs men,[45] it was edgy, smouldering, now and then breaking briefly into flame.

Richard Clark, of the customs house, lived in School Street near the King's Chapel, Boston, and one morning—an odd time!—all of his windows were smashed.

The comptroller of customs of Falmouth, Massachusetts,[46] was awakened one night at pistol point and made to name an informer. The informer, informed, escaped.

Thirty-odd men, their faces blackened, took over a revenue schooner near Philadelphia and released its prize, a small vessel loaded with tea, claret, gin.

A press gang from H.M.S. *Rose* under Lieutenant Henry Panton boarded the fishing vessel *Pitt Packet* of Marblehead as she was returning home, and tried to take off Michael Corbet and three others who they said were deserters from the Navy. The four denied this, and barricaded themselves in the forecastle. Corbet had a harpoon. "If you come down here," he called to Panton, "I'll kill you." So Panton went down, and Corbet killed him. Corbet was tried for murder on the high seas, James Otis and John Adams defending him, and was acquitted on a technicality.

That same Otis, the fiery orator, the pamphleteer par excellence, was not to be in the ranks of the effective patriots much longer. He had been acting queer for some time; but after he tangled with Robinson of the Boston customs commissioners in the British Coffee House in King Street, September 5, 1769, and was hit over the head with the flat of Robinson's sword, he was never the same again and had to turn over the active leadership to Samuel Adams.[47]

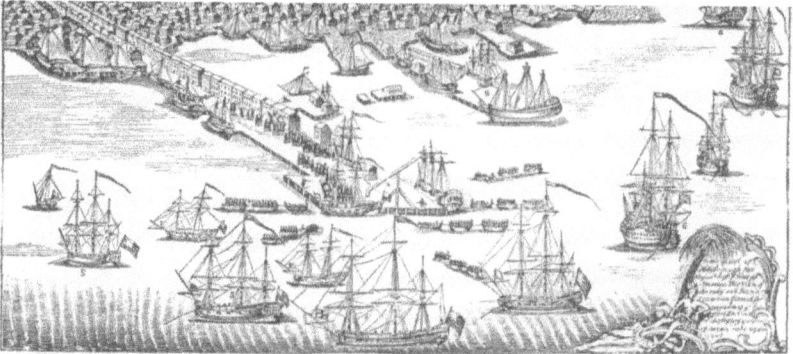

5. THE LANDING OF BRITISH TROOPS AT BOSTON, 1768

Ebenezer Richardson, another customs man, was set upon by a crowd of boys in Boston the afternoon of February 22, 1770, and took refuge in the home of a friend, Theophilus Lillie. There he lost his head and fired wildly from an upstairs window, killing eleven-year-old Christopher Snider. The boy was given a tremendous funeral, half the town attending. Richardson was tried and found guilty, but he was pardoned by Acting-Governor Hutchinson, and the service sent him to Philadelphia, where he was fondly pointed out as Murderer Richardson.

Hutchinson was acting governor because Francis Bernard had returned to England. This was considered a victory of the radicals, who for some time had been clamoring for his removal from office, and who celebrated his sailing with fireworks, flags, and a parade. However, Bernard was *not* recalled in disgrace, but rather was created a baronet. The Whigs only made it seem a Whig victory because they were woefully short of victories just at that time. Moreover, in Thomas Hutchinson, the lieutenant governor, they got a chief who disliked them at least as much as Bernard had, and feared them less.

Hutchinson took a gloomy view of the situation in Boston, for though he firmly believed that the mass of the people preferred peace and quiet he knew that the radicals were well organized and that they would never pause, much

less quit. The sending of the soldiers—or of so few of them—
he knew was a mistake. And he was being proved right, every
day.

The soldiers had been landed in the bay under the guns of
warships and while they had not been resisted neither had
they been welcomed with anything like warmth. When they
asked that quarters be assigned to them they were coldly if
correctly told that the town or province did not have to
provide private quarters unless there were no appropriate
public quarters available. What was the matter with Fort
William?

Well, what was the matter with Fort William was that
it was three miles by water from downtown Boston and as
such was not a handy place from which to sally forth from
time to time to keep order; but General Gage, who attended
the landing in person, raised no splutter. This was to character-
ize the whole "occupation." The military knew that they were
not wanted, and they behaved with a fixed, unwavering
propriety. On this occasion half the men went to Fort William,
though they were moved soon afterward to Faneuil Hall.
The other half pitched camp right there on the Common.

The customs commissioners and their sundry underlings
emerged from Fort William, where they had gone after a few
days aboard the *Romney*, and they moved back to their town
offices, which were guarded night and day by redcoats. This
emphasized the connection if an emphasis was needed.

Even if it had not been for the angry voice of coercion,
which was bound to be sounded, no matter how exemplary
the visitors were in their behavior, the Bostonians would have
hated them. This was inevitable.

Suspicion of a standing army, of professional soldiers,
went back many centuries among the English-speaking peoples,
but it had always been especially virulent in the American

mainland colonies, where the old-fashioned idea prevailed (and it was old-fashioned even in the eighteenth century) that every man should be his own family's protector, ready to seize a weapon and go forth and give battle at a moment's notice. What else did any man require save courage and a hornful of powder? Membership in the militia was compulsory, and that was that. If they knew how to mold bullets, and if they could do their drill once a month or so on the green, what else could anybody ask? They didn't need epaulettes, sabretauches, cartouches, cockades, pipeclayed crisscross belts. You take a full-time soldier, now, and no matter how fancy you dress him up, no matter how many plumes and how much froggery you might fasten onto him, what, after all, was he? He was a hired killer, that's what he was. He was a man who murdered because he was paid to.

There were other, more personal reasons.

The British Army was made up at this time of three strictly blocked-off classes.

The officers, though they did not always let this show, were gentlemen. Commissions were not won, but bought. Promotion too was largely a matter of purchase, and most of the officers would stay where they were unless they performed some extraordinarily brilliant feat—or unless their relations advanced them more money. Some of the officers loved their lot, some of them hated it. You never knew what an officer was going to be like.

The sergeants and corporals were the true professionals. To them the Army was a way of life, and they made it run. They were durable, and utterly dependable. They did not aspire ever to become officers: that would have been improper, even if it was possible.

The rank-and-file were unspeakable. No more than the non-coms would dream of becoming officers would the average private dream of becoming anything higher than private. Here and there one might find that he had encountered his calling, that he was a soldier born, and such a one, a pearl, soon would become a sergeant. But by and large the British soldier was a brute, and he was treated like a brute, not to be trusted by his superiors or even by his fellow brutes, and most assuredly not by civilians.

There had been no thought of enlisting. Extremest poverty might drive a man into the Army, but more often he had to be tricked or forced in. He woke up one morning with a hangover and was told that he had inadvertently taken the King's shilling in the course of the party the previous night, and that now he was in for it; or else he was found guilty in court of any one of the scores of capital crimes and quite bluntly given a choice between the Army or a noose— and likely enough he afterward regretted that he hadn't chosen hanging.

Life for the rank-and-filer was unbelievably harsh. The threat of the noose might be gone, temporarily at least, but in most outfits savage floggings were an everyday occurrence. They were invariably public. In Boston they were performed —blood, torn flesh, and all—right out in the Common. And there were a great many of them. For all the scorn with which the countryman professed to hold the military manual of arms —"the discipline" it was called then—he sensed that there was some mystery about it and that he and his fellows would become better men if they could somehow penetrate this mystery. In consequence, the redcoats, when they *did* get a chance to fraternize for a few minutes with visitors from out of town—which was seldom—were swamped with invitations to desert and to take a cushy post as drillmaster in some remote western Massachusetts village. The prospect was enticing; and in the beginning dozens of them, always looking for a chance to escape from the Hell in which they found themselves, accepted. There were more than forty the first month. Practically all of these were recaptured, and all of the recaptured ones were publicly lashed to within an inch of their wretched lives. Finally, reluctant though they were to lose an able-bodied man—for they were always short-handed and they could not expect to pick up any recruits, by whatever methods, in this benighted land—they shot a man. This too was done right out on the Common. The barbarians must learn how a civilized army acts.

For the most part the soldiers and the civilians were never allowed to come into contact. The officers, commissioned and otherwise, saw to that. Nor were the men ordinarily permitted to walk the streets alone. That was too dangerous. Such a pedestrian could be belted with garbage, or he could be rushed from behind by men who threw him on his face in the mud or even pitched him into some pond. "Lobsterbacks" they were called, when they weren't called something much worse.

They could answer back, if not with blows—these were forbidden—at least with profanity; and this they frequently did do.

> *Yankee Doodle came to town*
> *Dressed in tightest trows-es,*
> *And vowed he could not see the place*
> *There was so many houses*

Bostonians were not, then, the unbending puritans that their ancestors had been, but they still held the Lord's Day in high respect, and it was just on that day that the redcoats took to singing. They would gather in groups before the doors of meeting houses where services were being held, and they would sing very loudly and not well.

Yankee Doodle keep it up,
Yankee Doodle dandy,
Mind the music and the step,
And with the girls be handy.

Most of the songs that they sang were not, like this, innocuous, only thinly satiric. Most of them were filthy.

It could not go on like that. Something, soon, was going to snap.

Monday, March 5, 1770, a raw wet night, something did.

17

BLOOD ON THE SNOW

AMERICAN LIBERTY was to be won with many weapons. The over-the-fireplace musket was the most familiar, and in the beginning was easily the commonest. It made a noise like a slammed door, had a terrific kick, threw a two-ounce chunk of lead, and could kill a man as far away as seventy or eighty yards—if the shooter was lucky enough to score a hit. For the musket was a wildly inaccurate gun. In conventional armies of the time, such as the British Army, "controlled fire" was everything. There was to be no individual shooting, only volleys. Indeed, the British Army's regulation musket, the Brown Bess, did not even have a rear sight, for the men were not taught to aim it, only to point it in the general direction of the enemy, turn their heads away (to avert the danger of a flareback at the touch-hole, which could burn a man's eyes out) and at the command of an officer tug at the trigger.

The over-the-fireplace muskets were of all weights and sizes, and of all calibers. Many were homemade. As the war wore on these were replaced by superior European military muskets, most of them French, smuggled in at first, sent openly after the alliance of 1778, until at last there was some semblance of uniformity and men in action could exchange ammunition as needed. There were also a few companies of riflemen in the Continental Army, most of them from western Pennsylvania; but the rifle, though it would carry farther and was admittedly much more accurate, took too long to reload to be useful in battle, so that it was employed only for sharpshooting and scouting.

Few pistols were used. The pistol was a duelist's toy rather than a soldier's friend-in-need. It would not carry half as far as a musket and was even less accurate. Its mechanism was too delicate for field conditions; and much of the time, even when it had been well cared for, it wouldn't go off at all. Officers protected themselves with their swords, or, better, with spontoons, which were sometimes carried by sergeants as well, in both the British and Continental armies. The spontoon was a half-pike or halberd, long enough to permit the officer to meet an onrushing musketeer with a bayonet on the end of his musket. The bayonet as a weapon was almost unknown in America at the beginning of the long struggle, and it was not until the French had sent over thousands of them, and French and German officers had spent many a weary hour instructing in their use, that the Continentals could see them as anything but meat skewers around a camp fire: by the end of the Revolution the Continentals were pretty good with the bayonet in battle. On the other hand, the British all that time were the best bayoneteers in the world. It was their special pride.

The indefatigable Benjamin Franklin was to propose, early in the Revolution, that the newly formed Continental Army make the long bow its primary weapon, rather than the musket; and he gave a number of good reasons for this;[48]

but the suggestion seems never to have been taken seriously.

Members of street mobs snatched up the nearest thing that looked at all lethal, stones being favored, or hastily cut cudgels, or, in the case of the coopers' apprentices, barrel staves; but the strangest and surely one of the most effective weapons in a melee, the rioter's delight, was—a wolder stick.

A wolder stick was made of hard wood, and it was about 3½ to 4 feet long. It was about 2 inches thick in the middle, this thickness tapering, very gradually, to about 1 inch at either end; and the ends were rounded. That is, it was like an oversized policeman's night stick.

The wolder stick was a necessity in the rope walks, or rope factories, that abounded in Boston. It was used as a sort of lever to regulate the angle of lay in making the larger, thicker rope. There were always plenty of them lying around, and they were easily replaced.

At the beginning of the year 1770 there were only two regiments stationed in Boston, the fourteenth and the twenty-ninth, plus a company of artillery, five cannons. There had been four regiments, for a while, the Sixty-fourth and Sixty-sixth having been brought down from Halifax; but lately Gage, thinking that he had the situation well in hand, had sent those latter two back to Nova Scotia; and indeed he was even thinking of removing all that remained—when Hell broke loose. Gage himself was back in New York then, his headquarters. New York seemed a likelier powder keg than Boston. On one of the first days of the new year the redcoats there, exasperated by the boastfulness of the local Sons of Liberty, had chopped down the Sons' prized Liberty Pole and sawed it up for firewood. This was too much—it was done deliberately, not by chance—and the Sons attacked; and in the ensuing fray one civilian was bayoneted to death. So Gage was in New York.

On the afternoon of Saturday, March 3, a private of the Twenty-ninth was passing John Gray's rope walk, right in the center of town, when one of the workers called out to ask him if he'd like a job. Thinking to make a little spending money [49]—the redcoats were miserably paid, when they were paid at all—this soldier stopped and said sure. "Then you can clean out my ——house," the worker called. "It's all you're good for."

The soldier invited him to come out in the street and say that again, which the worker did; and they started to fight. Friends of the soldier came on the run, but the workers at the same time swarmed out of the rope walk—and *they* had wolder sticks. The battle wasn't a long one. The soldiers, perforce, broke and ran.

This was only one scene of violence among many—for there had been bad blood between the soldiers of the Twenty-ninth and the John Gray rope makers for some time—but somehow it seemed destined to be the telling one. Somehow all over Boston it was being whispered that the big fight would come next, the fight to end them all. Not the following day, no, for that was the Lord's Day; but maybe Monday? Yes, it would probably be Monday night.

Monday night, sure enough, that same neighborhood, near the customs house, was crowded with small prowling parties of artisans looking for trouble. The troopers of the Twenty-ninth were confined to barracks, near the Brattle Street Church. It was the Fourteenth's night for guard duty.

It was a nasty night, cold, wet, the streets covered with snow and ice and frozen clods of mud. There was a young moon to the north, very low.

In Dock Square a mysterious stranger (he never was identified) in a white wig and red cape harangued a restless crowd for perhaps ten minutes; but nothing happened immediately afterward, except that more and more citizens kept appearing all the time. Somebody started to ring a church's bell, and many of those who came to King Street thought that they were answering a fire alarm.

At King Street and Royal Exchange Lane, before the customs house, was a single Fourteenth Regiment sentry, Hugh White by name. At about nine o'clock a Captain Goldfinch came along, and the sentry saluted him, as he had been taught to do. A small boy nearby, a barber's apprentice, Edward Garrick, jeered at the captain and saucily asked him why he hadn't paid to have his hair dressed.

The captain ignored the boy and passed on, but the sentry, White, made a show of chasing the boy away, and according to Edward he even poked him between the shoulderblades with the butt of his musket, causing him to fall to his knees. Then the sentry went back to his post. The boy ran off.

A few minutes later the boy was back, surrounded now by sympathizing grownups. He stabbed a forefinger at sentry White. "There's the son of a bitch that knocked me down," he cried.

The crowd edged in, muttering ominously. There were no guns among them, but there were sticks—but no *wolder* sticks—and there were snowballs packed firmly around rocks. "Fire, I dare you to!" they cried, pelting him with snowballs as they did so. "Go ahead, shoot!"

They had been told, and everybody in Boston believed, that the soldiers could not possibly fire their guns, even in self defense, unless authorized to do so by a civilian magistrate, something that no magistrate would dare to do.

White became rattled, and he ran up the customs house steps. At the top he paused to load his musket. (Why the musket was not loaded in the first place is not clear, but it could have been leaning-over-backward orders from officers

6. THE BOSTON MASSACRE

determined to avert all trouble, or it could have been because a loaded musket in the hands of a nervous man who might be jostled could easily go off by accident. For routine sentry purposes, anyway, White's bayonet would be enough deterrent.)

The crowd did not follow White, but still he couldn't get away. There might have been fifty or sixty of them, with more coming all the time.

A Captain Thomas Preston in the nearby barracks heard that a brawl was brewing, and he dispatched a sergeant and six privates—and *their* muskets were loaded—and followed them to the scene a few moments later, when he had strapped on his sword.

White ventured down the steps.

Preston tried to reason with the crowd, but he could not make himself heard. He placed himself between the crowd and his own men, a position of great peril. The gap was getting smaller at every moment.

"Fire! Go ahead and fire!"

Preston was to swear to his dying day that he had not given an order to fire, and had not even thought of such a thing, but so many others were crying out the word that inevitably a soldier got mixed up—and did fire.

Then they all fired. The noise was terrific.

When the smoke rolled away, an instant later, it was seen that eleven men lay in the street. Some were twitching, some were still. From all came great gouts of blood, blood that was a brilliant red against the snow.

CHAPTER

18

NO SICILIAN VESPERS

A MAN HIT by a musket ball at more than a hundred yards might not even know it. "Spent balls" were no more harmful than pebbles. They might tear the clothing; but they seldom got as far as the skin.

Up close it was different. The huge bullets knocked men right over backward, making enormous wounds. When fired from nearby they did not just chip bones: they smashed bones to smithereens.

A battlefield right after the fighting has stopped never is a pleasant sight—or smell. In the eighteenth century it must have been particularly appalling.

The smoke drifted sluggishly away. The townsmen disappeared, finding whatever shelter they could. The soldiers, trembling, frightened by the sight of what they had done, reloaded.

The townsmen came back. They only meant to carry off those who had fallen, but to the soldiers, bordering on panic, it looked like a counterattack, and they would have let loose with another volley had not Captain Preston passed among them knocking up gun barrels.

123

Three men were dead. Two, indubitably, were dying. Others had been hurt: one man, an innocent bystander, was to lose an arm.

Boston was in a turmoil. It seethed. Men were babbling questions. Men were running around crying for guns, guns, guns of any sort. You could not face firearms with only a barrel stave in your hands.

Everywhere men were saying that this was It. This was the Real Thing. It had happened at last. Bostonians would not have to tackle it alone, either; for there were reports that militiamen were pouring in from Roxbury, Cambridge, Charlestown, all around.

In his rebuilt house in Court Street Acting-Governor Thomas Hutchinson was faced by hand-wringers who wailed that this was open insurrection, chaos, a fight to the death. Hutchinson was fifty-nine and fearless. All unattended, he went out into the street, word speeding ahead of him that he would speak to the crowd from the Town Hall. He could not get to the front steps of that structure, the crush was so great, but by an alley he reached the back door, and soon he was addressing the crowd from a second-story window. He begged its members to disperse. He promised them that justice would be done, no matter what the cost, no matter what the provocation. He would start his inquiry right then and there, he said.

He was disliked, but he was respected. He was heard.

A full company of redcoats had been summoned from the barracks, on the double. Their muskets were loaded and ready; their bayonets were ready; and so were they. Each on one knee, the so-called "street-firing" position, they formed a wide half-circle before the customs house. They were under the strictest orders not to shoot until they heard a clear command —from *behind* them—to do so.

It was touch-and-go for an hour or more, the crowd sullenly surging back and forth, the soldiers tense, muskets cocked. At last the townsmen began to fall away, though at least a hundred of them stayed on the scene all night.

In the Town Hall, Acting-Governor Hutchinson sat as a court with two civil magistrates lately yanked from their homes. They heard Captain Preston. They heard each of the soldiers in the squad. They heard sentry White. They heard the two commanding officers, Lieutenant Colonel William Dalrymple of the Fourteenth, Lieutenant Colonel Maurice Carr of the Twenty-ninth. The hearing took more than three hours, and it was almost dawn when the court rose.

Preston and each of the eight soldiers, including the sergeant, were put under arrest—for their own protection.

Hutchinson was back on the job at nine o'clock. In nearby Old South Church a special town meeting was in progress, but there were thousands who could not get in and who waited, open-mouthed, in the streets outside. Many of these had come from far away. They were ready to fight. Would they be asked to? It depended upon the town meeting.

Sam Adams emerged; and the crowd fell silent.

Never a man to raise his voice if he could make his point in an undertone, Adams leaned toward those nearest him and said quietly: "Both regiments or none. . . ." He repeated this many times as he made his way through the crowd to the Town House, where the Acting-Governor, the provincial council, and others were waiting for him. "Both regiments or none. . . ." The crowd quickly picked it up, passing it back and forth. Samuel Adams went into the Town House, where he confronted Thomas Hutchinson.

How those two hated one another! Hutchinson was heavy-jowled, scowling, haggard with anxiety, a puritan of puritans, all quivering conscience, yet bound that he would not be budged. Adams, with his twitching mouth and twitching hands, his steel-gray eyes, his slovenly clothes, was a man haloed by triumph. He had waited a long while for this break of luck.

He voiced the demand of the town meeting. The people in the street outside already were chanting that demand, so that it seemed almost to rock the building where the officials sat. "Both regiments or none. . . . Both regiments or none. . . ." Hutchinson refused.

Hutchinson sat alone. The Council to a man advised him to give in, and so did both commanding officers, and even the provincial secretary, his brother-in-law, Andrew Oliver. It meant open war if he didn't, they said. They could have been right.

"Both regiments or none. . . ."

It swelled. Only a chant at first, now it was thunderous.

Acting-Governor Hutchinson as last submitted. He signed an order committing both the Twenty-ninth and the Fourteenth to Fort William.

These regiments were thereafter to be known, on both sides of the sea, as "Sam Adams' regiments." They did not like the name.

The customs commissioners and all their clerks and assistants and inspectors and spies of course immediately went to the same fort. They would not have been safe in the city without those troops.

Sam Adams' victory had been clear-cut, and this was perhaps his most glorious hour; but he was not to have everything his own way. Vocally and in print, he clamored for an immediate trial of the prisoners.

Hutchinson refused. A trial at that time would have been far from fair. Samuel Adams yammered, a maniac; but the Governor had given in far enough, and again he said no.

Sam's second cousin, John, had better sense. He had been in Boston the night of the shooting, though he had taken no part in it, but rather had hurried back to Braintree to make sure that his beloved Abby and his children were safe. Nobody knew what might happen that night. No Caucus Club radical, John Adams nevertheless stood pronouncedly on the side of the patriots, and it jolted him, next day, when he was asked to undertake the defense of Captain Preston. He thought. He accepted, taking one guinea as an advance payment against his fee. A gloomy man by nature, he was especially gloomy about this decision. It would mean the end of his political career, he believed. It would mean that he would be jeered at and spat upon in the streets—as to be sure he was. But it was the right thing to do, so he did it.[50]

Another prominent patriot, young Josiah Quincy, also accepted an appointment to the defense counsel. The third was a Tory, Robert Auchmuty, who, in the opinion of Captain Preston himself, was the best of the lot.

The four dead men (the fourth had died next day and a fifth was to die soon) were buried in a common grave near the northeast corner of the Granary Burying Grounds, the ceremony being attended by thousands.

The customs house in King Street thereafter was to be called, by townsfolk, Butchers' Hall. The affair itself was to go down in the history books under the somewhat inflated name of the Boston Massacre. It was, in truth, no Sicilian Vespers, no St. Bartholomew, or Glencoe; but it did, duly exploited, loom large in the emergence of American liberty.[51]

The barracks at Fort William had been put up for one regiment only, nor was it possible to enlarge them when nobody would sell the soldiers building materials or would work for them as carpenters; so that now, what with the two regiments, the original garrison, and all of the members of the customs crew, the place was certainly uncomfortable and quite possibly unsanitary. Gage, in New York, wrote to Hutchinson, offering to transfer one or both regiments. Hutchinson, rather pathetically, refused.

"I am absolutely alone, no single person of my Council or any other person in authority affording me the least support and if the people are disposed to any measure nothing more is necessary than for the multitude to assemble, for nobody dares oppose them or call them to account," he wrote. "I could not justifie, at such a time, moving to send the Kings troops out of the province." [52]

The trial of Captain Preston was started in Massachusetts Superior Court October 14, after a long cooling-off period. It lasted until October 30, the first criminal trial in the history of the colony that had gone for more than one day. Samuel Quincy and Robert Treat Payne [53] prosecuted. The result was an acquittal; and there was no demonstration.

The eight soldiers directly accused, together with four others who were alleged to have fired from upstairs in the customs house building, had petitioned against a separate trial for Captain Preston, believing as they did that they would have a better chance if they were tried with him; but this had been disallowed.

Counsel for the prosecution was the same, but Sampson S. Blowers had replaced Judge Auchmuty in defense counsel. The trial of the original eight lasted from November 27 to December 5, and resulted in the acquittal of all excepting Hugh Montgomery and Matthew Killroy, who had been proved, the court thought, to have deliberately aimed and fired at certain persons, rather than to have fired in wild self-defense, like the others. These two were allowed to plead guilty of the lesser charge of manslaughter. They were released when they had established their "clergy"—their literacy—by "reading" from the Bible the so-called "neck verse," the Fifty-first Psalm, which they had been careful to memorize. The only punishment inflicted was not, properly, a punishment at all. In order to prevent them from again pleading their "clergy," if they should happen to get into more trouble, Killroy and Montgomery, in accordance with a quaint old English custom, were branded on the brawn of their left thumbs.

The case against the four soldiers who were supposed to have fired from the customs house was so palpably unproven that the jury did not even go out: it simply *waved* its dismissal.

CHAPTER

19

A SCHOONER IS BURNED

THE REACTION in England was curious. There was little indignation that British troops had fired upon and killed British citizens but a great deal of indignation that British troops had been ordered to an out-of-the-way spot because of the demands of a colonial rabble. Mobs were nothing new to Englishmen, in particular to Londoners, but bossing the Army around was. It seemed unnatural, even indecent.

The Massacre would not soon be forgotten, but immediately it raised less dust than might have been expected. The Sons of Liberty could hardly ask for anything *more*, Englishmen cried. In Boston the Caucus Clubbers were vastly disturbed by reports that Parliament was about to invoke a law that dated back to Henry VIII giving the Crown the right to haul any person back into England proper for trial for treason, and it was rumored that Sam Adams, John Hancock, and Thomas Cushing were marked for such treatment, and also by reports that the ministry in London was taking definite steps to have colonial governors and judges paid by the Crown. Others were not so deeply stirred.

The first would surely have raised a fuss if there had been any real reason to take it seriously, but the leaders in question were to be seen in the streets and taverns every day, and though there had been discussion of such a move in the House of Commons—where even so stern a proponent of severity toward the colonies as George Grenville spoke against it— it was perfectly understood that this was nothing but talk, just empty threats.

The second, in the nature of it, was a purely political matter and did not disturb the average citizen. Town meetings were called in Boston, but they were not well attended. They petitioned the new governor, Thomas Hutchinson, whose formal commission had recently come across the sea, together with the commission as lieutenant governor of his secretary and brother-in-law, Andrew Oliver, asking for information about this salary matter; and the Governor replied, with his accustomed bad temper, that he was not obliged to give out information about his instructions from Home. Otherwise little enough was done, anywhere.

The non-importation movement wavered, but it had stung the British merchants, and only a month after the Boston Massacre, without fanfare, almost without comment, Parliament repealed all of the various Townshend acts excepting the one that taxed tea. True, there was a preamble to the repealer that asserted again Parliament's right to tax the colonies, and Lord North, who seldom ceased to be circuitous, even for a moment, said, straightforwardly: "I am for retaining our right of taxing America." But then, there had been the Declaratory Act at the time of the Stamp Act repeal, and what did *that* amount to?

As for tea, the colonists already, by means of an ingenious device written into the original bill in order to get them to like it, were buying that, by way of London and the East

India Company auctions, at nine pence a pound less than their heavily taxed English cousins were obliged to pay for it. Even so, the Americans preferred to buy smuggled tea, which was cheaper yet. They got this from Dutch vessels, sometimes directly, sometimes by way of the West Indies; for the Netherlands was another nation that had large Oriental holdings as well as many ships and seamen.

This preference hurt the East India Company, which had a monopoly on all tea taken from the Far East to England, and which was staggering, rocking on its heels. Nabob after nabob came back from India to set up a sumptuous household at Home, but the mismanagement was scandalous, and in order to keep the stockholders quiet the directors as recently as 1766 had raised dividends from 6 per cent to 10 per cent—and that smack in the face of an adverse financial report. However, none of this troubled the Americans, who continued to buy Dutch tea. *They* were not investors in the East India Company.

As early as September of that year 1770, the *St. James' Chronicle* [54] was reporting that bets in the City were eight to three that even the stubborn Bostonians would be importing from the mother country again before the end of October. They were right. The break came in August, in New York, and within a very short time the whole non-importation movement had quietly collapsed.

It was hard to stay angry, just at that time. Hillsborough had been forced out of the secretaryship of state for colonial affairs, to be replaced by Lord Dartmouth, an amiable minister, a minister all unbrushed by the Hillsborough hauteur, one who was moreover reported to be friendly toward the American colonies, though still a "King's Man." There was a feeling that the worst might have been passed. There was a great deal of high hope to this effect, hope that the two sides of the sea could thereafter work well together, and this was shared by such sincere American patriots as Joseph Warren, Benjamin Franklin, and, in his more lucid moments, James Otis.

The so-called *Gaspee* incident did much to shatter this.

The *Gaspee* was an eight-gun schooner attached to the ship-of-war *Beaver* and assigned to the waters of Narragansett Bay and Long Island Sound. She was commanded by a lieutenant named William Dudingston, who took his responsibilities very seriously indeed. Dudingston was a pest. He hailed everybody, stopped everything, searched everywhere. He cause exasperating delays, and did it in an arrogant manner. What he seized he sometimes sent to Boston, to be adjudged in the vice-admiralty court there, much to the inconvenience of local Rhode Island traders, some of whom got together and petitioned the governor, Joseph Wanton, to do something about it.

Governor Wanton wrote, respectfully enough, to Dudingston, asking to see his credentials. Question a British Naval officer? It was like questioning angels in Heaven. Wanton got two answers, each more or less a snarl; and then Dudingston, in high dudgeon, sent the correspondence to his superior officer, Rear Admiral John Montagu.

Montagu, member of a politically powerful family, was Dudingston all over again, only more so.[55] He was in charge of coastal waters all the way from Nova Scotia to the Floridas, and directly under him he had a fleet of twelve warships that had put in at Boston ostensibly to make preparations for a possible war with France, actually, as everybody knew, as a show of force, to keep the colonists in line. Montagu was no diplomat. He and his wife, who was if possible even more imperious, were heartily disliked in Boston.

Montagu wrote harshly to Governor Wanton, a letter in which he said nothing about Dudingston's credentials but spluttered instead about a plot he said he had heard of—he did not say how—to outfit a vessel and man it, in Newport, for the purpose of rescuing any prize Dudingston might take. "Let them be cautious what they do; for as sure as they attempt it, and any of them are taken, I will hang them as pirates," wrote the doughty admiral.

Dudingston went on chasing vessels, overtaking them, annoying them. On the afternoon of June 9, 1772, he was heading up the river from Newport to Providence, where he was to pick up some sailors being sent overland from Boston, for Dudingston was shorthanded at the time. He sighted a packet, bound the same way, and he cracked on extra canvas. The wind was at the north, so they had to tack. The skipper of the packet, Benjamin Lindsey, had of course recognized the schooner—every skipper in those waters knew the odious *Gaspee* on sight—and he assumed that Dudingston was chasing him, as perhaps Dudingston was. Off Namquit Point, about eight miles south of Providence, Dudingston's helmsman shaved it too close, and the schooner went aground. She was in no real trouble there, as Lindsey knew, but she would not be able to kedge off until the coming of high tide at three o'clock the next morning: Lindsey knew this too. Lindsey kept going, and when he reached the city, at sundown, he sought out John Brown, the richest merchant in town and a man who had personal as well as business reasons for disliking William Dudingston and the *Gaspee*.

Brown agreed that here was too good an opportunity to miss. "The Lord has delivered the Amalekites into our hands," he might have cried. He acted fast. He sent out a man to assemble longboats off Fenner's Wharf, a public dock opposite James Sabin's ordinary and to see that the oarlocks were muffled; and he sent a boy out with a drum to beat up the town with a cried announcement that all who wished to share in the destruction of the *Gaspee* should report promptly, with weapons, at Sabin's. It was as open, as public, as that.

They remained at Sabin's, molding bullets in the kitchen and making other preparations, until about ten o'clock, to let it get good and dark—there would be no moon that night—and then they crossed to Fenner's Wharf, seventy or eighty of them, and took to the boats. There were eight boats, each propelled by five pairs of oars. At the steering oar of each was a full-fledged skipper; and in charge of the whole expedition was Captain Abraham Whipple, the same who in the French and Indian War had commanded the phenomenally successful privateer *Game Cock*.

They reached the stranded *Gaspee* a little after midnight. She showed a light, sure evidence that they were not expected. They were within a few hundred yards before they were hailed.

"Who comes there?"

They made no answer but drove on, right for the bows of the schooner.

The lieutenant was summoned, and he scrambled topside in his nightshirt, a pistol in one hand, a cutlass in the other. He too challenged.

"Who comes there?"

Abraham Whipple then gave him the benefit of gale-hardened lungs:

"*I am the sheriff of Kent County, God damn you. I've got a warrant for your arrest, God damn you. So surrender, God damn you!*"

This was a lie, but it was a lie couched in language that Lieutenant Dudingston could understand. It might have saved some fighting. One of the schooner's bow guns was shotted, but already it was too late to use it, with the Yankees right under the bows: it could not be depressed that far. In a trice the schooner was swarming with armed men.

The tars, tumbling out of the forecastle, not knowing what it was all about, put up almost no resistance. A few of them were banged about a bit, that's all. Their hands were wired behind them, and they were pushed below hatches and locked there.

Dudingston either fired or started to fire, when he was cut down by a musket ball that clipped his left forearm and plowed into his left groin about five inches below the navel. It must have been a very painful wound, and it certainly was bloody—it gushed. They carried him down to his cabin, where Dr. John Mawney, one of the raiders, bandaged him as best he could, using the lieutenant's own linen. Mawney had not brought a bag. He was there as a fighter, not as a physician.

The tars were told that they could take as much of their personal belongings as they could carry. In most cases this meant all. They were bundled into boats and shoved off. The lieutenant was rowed to the Stillhouse Wharf at Pawtuxet, a few miles away, and left there—with men who could summon a surgeon.

The *Gaspee* was burned right down to her water line, and the next morning nobody knew how it had happened.[56]

Dudingston wrote to Montagu. Montagu exploded and wrote to Wanton. Wanton wrote back to Montagu, enclosing a copy of the gubernatorial proclamation he had been quick to issue, offering a reward of £100 for information leading to the arrest and conviction of any of the "perpetrators of the said villainy," and also enclosing some of the first depositions to be taken. There were to be scores of depositions. There were to be basketsful of them.

King George himself issued a proclamation offering a reward of £500 to any informer who would break the case, with the promise that if the said informer had himself been a member of the raiding party he would be fully and unqualifiedly pardoned.

Nobody came forward.

The Crown appointed a royal commission to inquire into the crime. It consisted of Governor Wanton of Rhode Island, the chief justices of New York, New Jersey, and Massachusetts, and the judge of the vice-admiralty court of Boston, that same Robert Auchmuty whose legal services Captain Preston had so warmly appreciated.

This commission first posted a notice pleading with any and all who knew about the affair to report what they knew. It first sat January 6, 1773, in Newport. It sat for two weeks, taking dozens of depositions from unimportant persons, and then adjourned to May, when it sat for almost two weeks more and took still further depositions.

It learned absolutely nothing.

20

A PUBLIC SPANKING

Benjamin Franklin was born in Boston, but this did not make him a Bostonian. In America, as he himself complained, he was called too English, whereas in England he was called too American. In the tortuous events that marked the Great Separation his attitude in general was middle-of-the-road, an attitude that caused extremists of both sides to distrust him. Right up until the end he went on hoping that the colonies and the mother country could be reconciled, and in his quiet way working for such a consummation.

Philadelphia was his home town, and he represented Pennsylvania in London for many years. He was also to represent New Jersey, Georgia, and Massachusetts. That last connection was not a happy one. Franklin never could resist a joke; there was always a twinkle in his eye; and his religious views were reputed to be, to say the least of it, liberal. This did not go down well with the "saints" of Massachusetts, the so-called "wise men of the East." Also, there was some reservation about his standing. When Lord Hillsborough became secretary of state for the colonies he refused to recognize

Benjamin Franklin as agent for the colony of Massachusetts Bay, for, he pointed out, though undoubtedly the Massachusetts House of Representatives had appointed him to that post the governor, Bernard, had refused to confirm the appointment. Franklin contended that Bernard had nothing to do with the matter, but Hillsborough, a stubborn man, was not moved. Not that it made any real difference. The post of agent was an unofficial one at best, an informal one, and Franklin's political influence, so gently applied, was far-reaching. Indeed, that influence was largely responsible for forcing Hillsborough out of the cabinet when Franklin saw how bad he was for the colonies, and it was Franklin who proposed his good friend Lord Dartmouth as Hillsborough's successor. Dartmouth, as soon as he became secretary of state, acknowledged Franklin as the agent for the Massachusetts House of Representatives.

Franklin was also, at this time, deputy postmaster general of the American colonies. He had re-organized that service and put it upon a paying basis for the first time in its history, and now it was running itself while Dr. Franklin stayed in London.

Everybody who knew him loved Benjamin Franklin. The man was irresistible. Yet politically he had enemies, for his wit, though not malicious, was barbed, and there were many pompous asses in public posts who did not enjoy being laughed at by an expert.

He was fond of practical jokes, preferably of a literary kind. His "Rules by Which a Great Empire May be Reduced to a Small One" caused many a laugh, but it caused some hard thinking too, for it was a brilliant exposition of the colonial case, none the less effective because it was done in deadpan; and there were those who resented it. His "An Edict by the King of Prussia" was hilarious, but more than one highly placed stuffed shirt took it seriously at first and was furious when others explained that it was a hoax.

The "Edict" purported to be exactly that. The King of Prussia stated that England had been settled by colonists from Germany—Angles, Saxons, Frisians, Jutes—who had never been emancipated. These had yielded very little revenue "to our august house," and therefore for the undoubted good of the said colonists the King was imposing duties on all goods exported from Britain or imported into it, and he stipulated that all ships to and from Britain must "touch at our port of Koningsberg, there to be unladen, searched, and charged with the said duties." There should be no more iron worked in England, and no more hats, but raw material might be sent to Prussia and there made up, "the people thus favoured to pay all costs and charges of manufacturing, interest, commission to our merchants, insurance, and freight going and returning." Moreover, the King of Prussia also decreed that "all the thieves, highway and street robbers, housebreakers, forgers, murders, s-d---tes, and villains of every denomination" be emptied out of the jails of Prussia and sent to England.

This too made him feared in certain circles.

These newspaper items were unsigned, but there was never any question about who had written them.

Early in the year 1772 Benjamin Franklin was allowed to look at ten letters addressed to the late Thomas Whately and written in 1768 and 1769 by Thomas Hutchinson and Andrew Oliver of Boston. Whately, a member of Parliament who had since died, as secretary to George Grenville when Grenville was chancellor of the exchequer was the principal author of the Stamp Act, though to Englishmen he was better known as the author of the classic "Observations on Modern Gardening."

These were private letters. How Franklin got them he was never to tell. When they were written Hutchinson had been lieutenant governor of the colony of Massachusetts and

Oliver had been the colonial secretary. These writers were now, since the resignation of Francis Bernard, respectively governor and lieutenant governor.

Franklin read the letters, pondered them, and sent copies to Thomas Cushing, speaker of the Massachusetts General Court, with the stipulation that they should not be made public. Then the roof fell in.

The letters—there were six by Hutchinson, four by Oliver—contained private opinions privately expressed. None of these opinions was new or startling. Oliver and Hutchinson had long been known as opponents of "levelling," proponents of the royal prerogative.

There are several possible explanations of why Franklin sent them to Cushing. He had not been in Massachusetts in many years and perhaps did not know the intensity of patriot feelings there and the relentlessness of the radical leadership: he might not have known, that is, that asking men like Hancock and Adams not to publish such letters—and at a time like this when they were desperately seeking something to exploit—was like asking starving men not to partake of a meal set before them. He might have done it because he thought it was his duty.[57] He might have done it to cause trouble, to precipitate a crisis.

The Caucus Club members did hold in for a little while, before they published the letters in full, but that only made the publication more exciting, as probably it was meant to do. Hancock from the floor dropped a dark hint that such letters existed, and out of doors Sam Adams muttered mysteriously about them. Very early they were viewed with horror by persons who never had read them. At last they were read to the whole General Court, the members of which, however, had previously been pledged to secrecy.

It was no use. Likely enough the radical leaders never

really meant to keep them quiet; but because of the delay, the publication of the letters to Whately came as an explosion.

It is hard to see, at this distance, why. Whatever else he might have been, Hutchinson was no hypocrite. He never strove to conceal his abhorrence of democracy. The most quoted sentence, "There must be an abridgment of what are called English liberties," if taken out of context, as it customarily was, did sound bad; but it was nothing new coming from Thomas Hutchinson. Nevertheless there was a hullabaloo. The legislature promptly petitioned for the removal from office of both men.

In England it was even worse. There the thing actually resulted in bloodshed. William Whately, a banker, brother of the late Thomas Whately, to whom the letters had been addressed in the first place, was accused by a former customs official, John Temple, of deliberately arranging to have them made public. He hotly denied this, calling Temple a liar. Temple challenged, and they met with both swords and pistols in Hyde Park, where Whately was badly wounded. The duel settled nothing. The same hard feeling remained, on both sides, and it was public knowledge that as soon as Whately was up and around the two meant to meet again in the park. This the pacific Benjamin Franklin did not wish to see happen, and he spoke up, confessing that it was he who had sent the letters to America—though he refused to say how he got them. This brought the lightnings around his head. He was called a sneak, a thief, a trickster.

Franklin had forwarded the Massachusetts legislature's petition for the removal of Oliver and Hutchinson to Parliament in August, but not until January was he summoned to appear before the Lords' committee of His Majesty's Privy Council for Plantation Affairs to be questioned about it. The petition was only an excuse, as those in the know were aware.

Word went out that the solicitor general, Alexander Wedderburn, a Scot noted for his scalding sarcasm, would be turned
loose upon the presumptuous American. This is just what
happened, and the chamber was crammed. Franklin was asked
only a few nominal questions, and then Wedderburn whirled
into what was obviously a prearranged tirade. He was savage.
He pounded the table. He shook his fists. He called Benjamin
Franklin every nasty name he could think of, and he had a
very nasty mind. Franklin, who was sixty-eight years old, had
to *stand* all through this—and it lasted almost an hour. He
showed no expression at all, and when at last he was contemptuously dismissed he went away without a word. After
that the committee, to nobody's amazement, rejected the
petition as "founded upon resolutions formed upon false and
erroneous allegations; and that the same is groundless, vex-
atious, and scandalous; and calculated only for the seditious
purposes of keeping up a spirit of clamor and discontent in
the said province."

Next morning—the papers clearly had been drawn up in
advance—Benjamin Franklin was formally notified that he
was no longer deputy postmaster general of the American
mainland colonies.

Wedderburn's behavior and language were so outrageous,
and Franklin's deportment was so dignified, that many who
had gone to the hearing in order to gloat, afterwards admitted
that their sympathy remained with the American. Nevertheless, it was plain that Franklin's usefulness as a colonial agent,
after that public spanking, was at an end; and he prepared to
return to America.

As for Wedderburn, he was elevated to the peerage.

21

TEA, TEA

Everybody in America drank tea. Rum was much favored, though other spirits, whiskey, gin, French brandy, were not unknown, and sometimes even water was drunk. Madeira could be found almost everywhere. Milk was largely confined to those who owned cows. Coffee and chocolate were citified drinks, effete, exotic, expensive. But tea was universally swallowed.

Even the Indian drank tea—when he couldn't get fire-water.

Tea was easily transported, easily prepared. It was stimulating and it was tasty. It was by no means fashionable, for its consumption was widespread. You could count on getting a good dish of tea just about anywhere in the colonies. It was *the* American drink.

Tea was the only article dutiable under the original Townshend acts that was not produced in England, and when the other duties were removed the tea duty stayed: it was a mere three pence a pound. Tea was taxed internally in England, but not in the colonies, where, as a consequence, it was cheaper. Though there were interlopers—and they were called just that—in theory the East India Company had an absolute monopoly on the importation of tea into England. It did not, however, have a monopoly on the *exportation* of tea *out of* England. This trade was open to independent dealers. The East India Company brought the stuff to London, easily the biggest tea port in the kingdom, for all practical purposes the only one, and there it was stored in warehouses and offered to dealers in periodic auction sales. The East India Company had nothing to do, directly, with America. Nonetheless, when the American colonists signed non-importation agreements in protest against the Townshend acts, the East India Company, still stunned and reeling from the costs of a war it had been waging in India, felt the pinch.

There was never any thought, in the case of tea, of the development of a colonial product, but sundry substitutes were from time to time proposed—and even tried. Something called "balsamic hyperion" was made out of dried raspberry leaves; and it was horrid. A thyme-based concoction was much used in Connecticut. Sage and sassafras and steeped catnip and even pennyroyal were courageously sampled.

Doubtless there were backslidings; and some secretly sipped real tea, smuggled or dutied; while certain merchants, who had promised not to, surreptitiously slipped packets of tea to favored customers, who were enjoined to keep it quiet. Brewing tea in coffeepots, for appearances' sake, was said to be a common method of evasion. All the same, consumption sank. The women, often brought together as Daughters of Liberty, organized non-tea parties; and large numbers of them signed something like this (the Boston form):

We, the daughters of those patriots who have, and do now appear for the public interest, and in that

principally regard their posterity, as such do with
pleasure engage with them in denying ourselves the
drinking of foreign tea, in hopes to frustrate a plan
that tends to deprive a whole community of all that is
valuable in life.

The press, which was overwhelmingly Whig, gave coin-
age to various disparaging names for the stuff that a little while
ago everybody had loved: "nauseous draught," "vile growth,"
"detestable weed," etc. Tea was said to be poisonous. It was
said to be fattening—also bad for the hair.

Old habit is hard to break, and the backsliding might have
increased, the merchants might have relaxed, the newspapers
could have moderated their somewhat hysterical attacks on
consumption of the "putrid Bohea," had not a pigheaded Parliament, at the bidding of a pigheaded King, who spoke
through his pigheaded but unfailing minister, Lord North,
early in May of 1773 suddenly agreed to extend the East India
Company's tea monopoly to America.

It was a measure not of oppression but of desperation.[58]
Something had to be done. So many great fortunes were rooted
in the East India Company, so many influential Englishmen
were shareholders, that the bankruptcy of that elevated outfit
would have been a national calamity, a disaster.

The company had 17,000,000 pounds of tea in storage in
London, with more coming all the time. It was not allowed
to sell retail, in England, but it could name an upset price at
its auctions, and it had recently raised this from two shillings
two pence a pound to two shillings four pence and then to
three shillings (tea sold from eighteen pence to two shillings
a pound in Holland, where there was no export duty), and
then expressed astonishment that there were so few takers.
Now an obliging Parliament knocked out both the drawbacks

and the export tax, lent the company £1,400,000 at a low rate
of interest, renounced the £400,000 a year the company had
been obligated to pay the government, and handed over control of the American market—without even mentioning this
to America.

Seemingly it never occurred to anybody in England that
the colonies might object to this. The duty of three pence a
pound had not been raised, and since the act eliminated a
middleman it would actually enable the East India Company
to lower the price to Americans so as to push out the Dutch
smuggling trade. Why, they should be delighted over there.

They weren't. They screamed bloody murder. The committees of correspondence, well-organized at last, and widespread, were for the first time in a long while given a live issue
to write to one another about; and this they exuberantly did.
The merchants *and* the smugglers—for both stood to lose—
joined with the Sons of Liberty.

Monopoly was nothing new in England—the East India
Company had been incorporated by Queen Elizabeth December 31, 1600—but America wanted no part of it. The record
of the English East India Company—there were lesser, not
connected French, Dutch, Scottish, Swedish, Spanish, and
Danish East India companies—was a record of violence, un-
paralleled arrogance, and greed. It stank in American nostrils.

The company handled more than tea. Its products included also pepper, shellac, silk, saltpeter, calico, muslin, and
china, and these made up about one-third of the colonies'
imports from Great Britain. Were *they* to be handed over as
a monopoly, one by one, or all together? Were *they* to pay
duty?

The company made it that much worse by the nature
of the men it named to receive the tea it meant to send to
America. Instead of seeking advice, and appointing established,

reputable, well-liked merchants, it played politics by picking men it believed would be acceptable to the gracious, giving government—in other words, Tories, the very persons the masses in America were increasingly associating with economic pressure. It named these in four seaports—New York, Boston, Philadelphia, and Charleston. It planned to build warehouses in those ports, and it had 1,700 chests of tea ready to go.

The Stamp Act lesson had been well learned. Clearly the way to defeat this new highhanded move on the part of the ministry was by going to those men appointed to receive the tea—consignees, they were called—and persuading them, by whatever means, to resign.

On October 15 the New York merchants thanked those skippers in port who, cagily, had refused in London to accept any of the disputed tea as cargo. And they talked the consignees—not amiably, but definitely, unmistakably—into agreeing that they would not touch the stuff when it arrived. The penalty, a common one at the time, would have been to be branded as "an enemy of the country," a label that could ruin any business man.

The very next day the Philadelphia merchants did the same thing. And soon afterward so did the merchants of Charleston.

In Boston it was to prove much harder.

The Boston consignees were Elisha Hutchinson and Thomas Hutchinson, Jr., the sons of the Governor; Richard Clarke and his son, relatives of the Governor; Benjamin Faneuil, Jr.; and Joshua Winslow. These were not men to be pushed around, and they said so.

CHAPTER

22

SO, THEY DO IT

Eᴀʀʟʏ ʀɪsᴇʀs in Boston one morning found that in the night the town had been plastered with handbills, reading thus:

> To the Freemen of this and the neighboring towns.
>
> GENTLEMEN,—You are desired to meet at Liberty Tree, this day, at twelve o'clock at noon; and then and there to hear the persons to whom the tea shipped by the East-India Company is consigned, make a public resignation of their office as consignors upon oath; and also swear that they will re-ship any teas that may be consigned to them by said company by the first vessel sailing for London.
>
> O. C., Secretary.
>
> Boston, Nov. 3, 1773.

☞ Show us the man that dare take down this.

The church bells were rung from eleven to twelve, and a goodly crowd was gathered, at least five hundred, at the appointed hour; but the consignees were not there.

The Liberty Tree, hung now with flags, was located in

the middle of a cleared space, known locally as "Liberty Hall," at the junction of Newbury, Orange, and Essex streets. There was no question about the awareness of the consignees that this strictly unlegal meeting was to be held: they had been awakened, individually, early in the morning, and served notices to that effect.

Boston, though one of the largest seaports in the New World, still was a small town. Everybody knew where the consignees were. They were in the Richard Clarke & Sons warehouse at the foot of King Street. A committee was appointed, consisting of William Molineux, William Dennie, Dr. Joseph Warren, Dr. Benjamin Church, Henderson Inches, Edward Proctor, Nathaniel Barber, Gabriel Johonnot, and Ezekiel Cheever, to wait upon them and insist that they resign. Molineux was the chairman.

This committee set forth at once, and virtually the whole meeting accompanied it, eager to see the fun. Everything was orderly, so far. As the procession passed the Town House Governor Hutchinson watched it from a window and marveled that so many of its members were "not of the lowest rank." Governor Hutchinson always was conscious of the lowest rank.

Richard Clarke & Sons occupied a two-storied wooden building. Downstairs was the warehouse, upstairs the counting-room or offices. The downstairs doors were open, but only the committeemen passed through them. They climbed the stairs.

They were challenged with: "From whom do you come?"

"From the whole people," Molineux replied.

The consignees, however, refused to recognize them or the legality of their act. Molineux, miffed, read aloud to them the resolution that the meeting had only now adopted, declaring them to be, if they did not resign, "enemies of the country." They had nothing to say to this.

The committee went downstairs and reported to the crowd in the street. There was an outcry. It was touch-and-go for a few minutes. The last thing the leaders wanted was another raging mob, another disgrace to the cause. Judge Nathaniel Hatch tried to quiet them, but he was jostled aside. Somebody indoors, downstairs, thinking that the premises were about to be invaded, started to lock the front doors, but the crowd foiled this by taking the doors right off their hinges and carrying them away. This was as far as the violence went, for after that the committeemen got the others under control.

Everybody went back to "Liberty Hall," where it was agreed that a meeting held informally out of doors *did* smack of turbulence. So a petition was addressed to the selectmen— with the Caucus Club organization this was easily done—who thereupon, as they were obliged to do, called a proper town meeting.

The meeting convened at Faneuil Hall at nine o'clock the next morning. It was a good meeting, an orderly one, with John Hancock as moderator. It passed a set of resolves similar to those passed a little earlier by a Philadelphia mass meeting. These were not hot, but they were firm. The meeting appointed a committee consisting of the moderator, Henderson Inches, Benjamin Austin, and the selectmen, to call more formally upon the consignees and again to demand that they resign. Then the meeting adjourned until three o'clock that afternoon, when the committee would report back.

The committee's report did not help. The Clarkes, father and son, and Benjamin Faneuil, had protested that they could hardly be expected to move without the concurrence of the Hutchinson sons, who were both at the Hutchinson summer home out in Milton, eight miles south of the center of Boston.

So still another committee—Hancock, Adams, John Pitts, Samuel Abbott, Dr. Warren, William Powell, and Nathaniel

Appleton—was named to go out to Milton and interview the obdurate Hutchinsons.

In all of this the radicals treated the Tories as though they were in truth Crown officials. Doubtless this was done in order to put them in a bad light. But it was not true. The consignees were, or were about to become—for they had not yet been named—employees of a private company, the East India Company of England.

The committeemen could not find Elisha Hutchinson, in Milton or in Boston, and the best they had been able to get out of Thomas, Jr., was a letter in which the Governor's son and namesake said that he and his brother did not think that they should do anything or promise anything until they had received official word of their appointments from London. The meeting did not like this. It smelled like stalling for time, which of course it was.

By now it was known from men on faster-moving vessels that the four ships [59] carrying tea to Boston already were on the way. When they arrived, if they unloaded the tea it would be in charge of the customs men for twenty days and then, if nobody came to claim it, and to pay duty on it, it would be offered to the public at an auction. If this happened it surely would happen under the protection of the troops, and the tea would be sold, the whole anti-tea movement would then be smashed, not only in Massachusetts but in all New England as well, in every one of the American colonies. The others depended upon Massachusetts.

Even if the tea was not unloaded, at the end of twenty days if duty had not been paid it would be up to the soldiers-protected customs men to seize it and offer it for sale. The only thing to do was send it back in the same ships, and the only way to do that was by causing the consignees to disclaim it.

The head of Richard Clarke & Sons was a very old man, and he had another son, Jonathan, who came from a visit to England on the morning of November 17, when there was a family reunion for him at the Clarke house near King's Chapel. This was interrupted by the arrival of a mob. It must have been a pickup mob, not ordered from above, for it seemed unsure of itself. Somebody on the second floor fired a pistol out of a window, but it did no harm: conceivably it had not been shotted. Many windows were broken, but the mob did not storm the doors, and soon their natural leaders came on the trot and talked them into drifting away.

Next day there was another town meeting, a notably quiet one. To it was read the final reply of the consignees to the demand that they resign:

> Boston, November 18, 1773.
>
> Sir,— In answer to the message we have this day received from the town, we beg leave to say that we have not yet received any order from the East India Company respecting the expected teas, but we are now further acquainted that our friends in England have entered into general engagements in our behalf, merely of a commercial nature, which puts it out of our power to comply with the request of the town.
>
> We are, sir, your most humble servants,
>
> RICHARD CLARKE & SONS,
> BENJ. FANEUIL, JR. for self and
> JOSHUA WINSLOW, Esq.,
> ELISHA HUTCHINSON, for my Brother
> and self.

Instead of the cries of indignation that might have been expected when this was read, the meeting silently accepted it and voted to dissolve. This terrified the consignees, as dire threats or bloodthirsty yells might have failed to do. As one man they petitioned the Governor to take over the tea when it came, relieving them of responsibilities they had not yet shouldered. He refused. It ill behoved a royal governor, he mentioned, to be taking possession of a private company's private shipment. Thereupon the consignees retired to the chill, sadly overcrowded Castle William.

On November 22 there was a joint meeting of the committees of correspondence from Boston, Dorchester, Roxbury, Brookline, and Cambridge. It was agreed that on no account should the tea be landed, and arrangements were made to send messages to other towns and to other provinces whenever the occasion would seem to call for such action. There was an air of grimness about this meeting.

Six days later, on November 28, the *Dartmouth*, with 114 chests of tea aboard, among other cargo, sailed into Boston harbor.

That was a Sunday, but such was the prevailing excitement that the selectmen held a special meeting anyway. They stayed in session until nine o'clock that night, hoping that the consignees would come to them. The consignees didn't.

The *Dartmouth* was ordered by the Sons of Liberty to tie up at Long Wharf, and her Captain Hall was instructed that on no account was any of the tea to be taken off. To see that these instructions were carried out a special guard was organized for the occasion, to keep watch night and day in shifts. This guard numbered from twenty-four to thirty-four on duty at any given time. They were armed with muskets and bayonets, and they kept military order, being, most of them, militia officers. They were not members of the rabble, but included such persons as John Hancock and Henry Knox, the fat bookseller.[60]

A mass meeting was called for the next morning. It was enormously attended, some 5,000 persons getting in or trying to get in, and it was moved from the usual Faneuil Hall to the nearby Old South Church, which was larger. It continued all that day and all of the next, Monday and Tuesday. At one time Sheriff Greenleaf, a moderate Tory, tried to break it up by reading a message from Governor Hutchinson who declared the meeting illegal and ordered it "to disperse and to surcease all further unlawful proceedings." He was hooted out of the hall. The meeting would never have heard him at all if it had not been for Samuel Adams' fervent plea for fairness. Adams figured that he could afford fairness now.

The customary resolutions were passed.

The second day the consignees wrote to John Scollay of the selectmen, and their letter was read to the meeting, still in session. They said that they had no right to send the tea back but that they were willing to store it until they could communicate with their employers-to-be and get further orders. Earlier, such a proposal might have at least received a hearing. The Boston town meeting of November 30 flatly refused even to consider it.

The *Dartmouth* was ordered from Long Wharf to Griffin's Wharf, and two other tea vessels, *Eleanor* and *Beaver*, which arrived within a few days, were ordered to tie up alongside of the first one. The same guard took care of all three.

Dartmouth was easily the most important. She had been the first, and what happened to her would happen to the others. The *Dartmouth's* twenty days would be up at midnight December 16. Her principal owner, the Quaker Francis Rotch, had promised to send her back if he could arrange to do so, and on December 11 he was haled before the Boston committee of correspondence, which had taken unto itself extraordinary powers, and asked why he had not lived up to his promise. He replied that the *Dartmouth* would be fired upon if she departed, Governor Hutchinson having urged Admiral Montagu to move the warships *Active* and *King-fisher* in such a way as to block the entrance of the bay to all unauthorized vessels; and this Montagu had done.

"The ship must go," pronounced Sam Adams. "The people of Boston and the neighboring towns absolutely require and expect it."

He was not presumptuous, this committee chairman, when he spoke for the neighboring towns. Committees of correspondence were writing in to Boston every day, from Cambridge, Roxbury, Charlestown, Malden, Newburyport, Lexington, Fitchberg, Gloucester, Leicester, approving the stand that at all costs the tea must not be landed.

The calls to meeting were waxing strident. On the morning of Tuesday, December 14, this was posted everywhere in Boston:

> Friends! Brethren! Countrymen! The perfidious act of your reckless enemies to render ineffectual the late resolves of the body of the people, demands your assembling at the Old South Meeting House, precisely at ten o'clock this day, at which time the bells will ring.

Once again Francis Rotch promised to do everything he could to obtain a clearance for the *Dartmouth*—*he* was certainly eager enough to get her out of port!—but the truth is he was being given a runaround by the customs collector and the comptroller, who passed the buck back and forth, while Governor Hutchinson left town. A young man named Copley, an artist, son-in-law of old Mr. Clarke, asked for a few hours to confer with the Clarkes, father and son; and this was granted. It took Copley longer, and he apologized, for he had been obliged to go all the way out to Castle William; and he accomplished nothing anyway. The meeting was adjourned until Thursday, December 16.

That was the telling meeting, since it must be the last one. Rotch was instructed to go out to Milton and beg the Governor—the only one who could, really—to give his vessel a clearance. He did so, in the rain, while thousands waited in Boston.

Thomas Hutchinson might have averted the scene that followed, but he did what he thought was right. He refused Rotch's request; and Rotch so reported back to the town meeting.

It was then that Samuel Adams rose in his place and said in a curiously loud voice: "This meeting can do nothing more to save the country." It was then that the "Mohawks" in the street let out their warwhoops and shook their hatchets at one another. It was then that the Boston Tea Party was launched.

23

AFTERMATH

THE DIE IS NOW CAST," said George III, who never had been noted for originality of phrase. "The colonies must either submit or triumph."

There was a great deal more than just £18,000 worth of tea involved here. If the thing had been done surreptitiously, or impulsively, or furiously by a mob, it might have gone down with lesser misdeeds, deplorable but not decisive. It was not so. "This Indian caper," as Admiral Montagu called it,[61] was planned weeks in advance; it was organized, engineered; and it was carried out calmly, swiftly, without a hitch. It was, indubitably, a direct act of defiance; and it must be met as such.

The one at Boston was not the only tea party—in New York a ship was turned back, and several chests of tea, the personal property of a skipper, were broken open and dumped into the bay; in Philadelphia the sight of a crowd of 8,000 convinced the captain of the *Polly*, carrying 697 chests, that he had better turn back, which he did; in Annapolis a brigantine was burned to the water line, tea cargo and all; in Charleston tea was permitted ashore, 257 chests of it, but nobody came to claim it and for three years it languished unused in a warehouse [62]—but Boston's was the most dramatic, the one that caught the imagination of the world. And now that world waited to see what Boston's punishment would be.

Nobody doubted that there would *be* punishment, and that it would be severe. The Boston Sons of Liberty had flaunted not only the might and majesty of the East India Company but the very might and majesty of the British throne itself. This must not pass unrebuked.

The Boston committee of correspondence had its jurisdiction questioned, but at a largely attended town meeting it was overwhelmingly endorsed and urged to go on with its work. Sam Adams still was chairman. By and large the merchants, in New York and Philadelphia especially, did not see any profit in continuing with non-importation; so Adams took the issue to the backcountry folks, drawing up what was styled (undoubtedly with Cromwell in mind) a Solemn League and Covenant, under which individuals pledged "in the presence of God, solemnly, and in good faith" to abstain from the purchase or use of any British manufactured article after October 1, 1774. The covenant caught on in central and western Massachusetts, districts that had not always in the past seen eye to eye with the Bostonians, and soon Adams could truthfully claim to represent the entire colony of Massachusetts Bay.

Governor Hutchinson wanted to go to England and see if he could not be of more help there, but on March 3 his brother-in-law Andrew Oliver, the lieutenant governor, had died; and it was not until the appointment of General Gage as governor, and Gage's arrival to take over the reins of authority, that Hutchinson was able to pack his things and depart, June 1.[63]

Gage arrived, with two extra regiments, May 13. Three

days before that the people of Boston had learned what their punishment was to be, at least as a beginner.

Parliament, summoned to a special session, had passed by large majorities three separate bills all aimed at Boston and at Massachusetts, which would be made an example of.

The first, the Boston Port Bill, which received the royal assent March 31, closed the port of Boston to all traffic until such time as the East India Company was paid for its tea and the various customs agents were reimbursed. The capital was moved to Salem, the customs house to Marblehead.

This of course spelled disaster. Boston was first of all a port. It lived by the sea, without which it would starve. In fact other towns and other colonies, from as far south as South Carolina, sent gifts of food to Boston, some of the merchants of which were able to carry on: twenty-eight merchants of nearby Marblehead, for example, offered the Boston merchants free warehouse space. But this could not continue. The other places would not go on supporting Boston indefinitely.

The second act revised by royal decree the whole charter of the colony. It provided that the Council should be appointed by the governor, as in most of the other colonies, and not elected by the people, as previously; that the selection of jurymen should be by the various sheriffs, not by popular vote, and that all sheriffs as well as all inferior judges should thereafter be appointed by the governor; and finally, and crushingly, that town meetings should be limited to one a year, as needed for the town financing, and should not be permitted even to discuss anything else. This cut the heart out of the carefully developed Massachusetts system of self-government.

The third act, though equally bad-tempered, was not at first so severe a blow, and it probably would have been the easiest to evade. It was designed, again, to strengthen the customs service. It provided, among other things, that any customs man who was charged with a crime committed in the performance of his duties could be tried in another colony or in England.

Soon afterward there was brought word of a fourth act—these acts were called "coercive" in Britain, "intolerable" in America—that, like the first three, had been passed by a big majority, and unhesitatingly assented to. This was the Quartering Act, and while it was painful it was not notably new, being no more than a much stricter Mutiny Act.

The colonists still had friends on the other side of the sea. In the Lords—for he was an earl now—William Pitt, Lord Chatham, thundered once more. "Keep your hands out of the pockets of the Americans and they will be obedient subjects," Colonel Barré had cried at the third reading of the Port Bill; and he and Gordon, Burke and Fox as well, had worked hard to get a repealer of the Tea Act: they were voted against 182 to 49. The mood of Parliament and of the ministry was unmistakable. There was to be no backing down this time.

"I know no line that can be drawn between the supreme authority of Parliament and the total independence of the Colonies," Thomas Hutchinson had told the Massachusetts General Court in the course of a carefully considered address, January 6, 1773; and to this the Court had replied: "If there be no such line, the consequence is, either that the colonies are vassals of the Parliament, or, that they are totally independent. As it cannot be supposed to have been the intentions of the parties in the compact, that we should be reduced to a state of vassalage, the conclusion is, that it was their sense, that we were thus independent."

That is, "independence" no longer was a dirty word. Men might mouth it openly. They were getting used to the sound of it.

There was to be one more face-slapping act, though it

had not been intended as such, and it came as though to top the climax. This was the Quebec Act, passed by that same Parliament in June. For the most part it was admirably framed and thought-out, but its timing was unfortunate.

For more than ten years, since the close of the war, Great Britain had been struggling with the problem of what to do with the French minority in Canada; and it had at last decided. In a burst of liberality it agreed to recognize Roman Catholicism there. Not only would it permit the celebration of the mass, but it would waive the Test Act in favor of a simple oath of allegiance, so that Catholics could actually serve in the government. It provided for trials without juries in civil cases, in accordance with an old French custom.

This was a good act, a farseeing act, carefully debated, and not aimed at the coastal colonies; but it made a kicked hornets' nest of New England. Throw out trial by jury? Surround us on three sides by papists? Here was an enactment *truly* intolerable—though the English did not class it and did not think of it as coercive.

The Quebec Act made for some additional hard feeling in the northern colonies, but it made no essential difference in the setup. The first four intolerable acts had been enough in themselves. Once again a stupid ministry and a stupid, ill-informed Parliament had come along at a crucial hour to save the American colonies by pulling them together. It couldn't have been better done if it had been directed from the Caucus Club at a regular meeting in the Green Dragon Tavern, Union Street, Boston, or in the counting-room of Chase and Speakman's distillery.

It gave the colonies a common complaint, a common fear, which was to result, very soon, in a Congress. The feeling was epitomized by a resolution passed by Hanover County,

Virginia (Patrick Henry's home), after news of the passage
of the Port Bill had been received:

> Whether the people there [at Boston] were war-
> ranted by justice when they destroyed the tea, we know
> not; but this we know, that the Parliament by their pro-
> ceedings have made us and all North America parties in
> the present dispute . . . insomuch that, if our sister
> Colony of Massachusetts Bay is enslaved, we cannot
> long remain free.

King George was right. The die had been cast. General
Gage, married to an American woman, himself an admirer of
America, had been assigned an impossible task. No matter how
many reinforcements they might send him, he would fail.
After the tea had been tossed into Boston Bay, Lexington and
Concord—and Bunker Hill—were inevitable.

NOTES

1. It is generally thought, though not proved, that this is the derivation of the American word "caucus," and it is certain that the calkers were among the first Boston worker groups to be organized, and that the Caucus Club, a strictly Whig, anti-Tory body, was for many years a powerful local influence. It has also been suggested, however, that "caucus" could have come from the Algonquin word "cau-cau-as 'u," or, as Captain John Smith spelled it, "caw-cawaasough," meaning one who advises, urges, encourages, from a verb meaning primarily to give counsel, urge, promote, incite to action. It is true, too, that many early American political clubs used Indian nomenclature. Tammany, for instance, was a Delaware chief; and to this day Tammany Hall is known, and not just jocularly, as the Wigwam, its rank-and-file as braves, its leaders sachems.

2. Now Pearl Street.

3. There was one exception. Major Thomas Melville, a hard-working businessman of Scotch birth, who lived at the corner of Green and Staniford streets, must have been other-

wise engaged when the order was given to empty footwear, for when he undressed that night he found his shoes full of tea, which he saved in a jar that was passed on down to his son and grandson, Herman, who "has attained popularity as an author." Drake, *Tea Leaves*, p. CXXXV.

4. The American phase of which was called the French and Indian War.

5. "There never did exist anything that may be called an accepted mercantile system, in the sense of an established body of mercantile doctrines upon which all the mercantilists could unite, for mercantilism never had any substructure of sound principles to support it. Opinion was constantly shaping and reshaping itself, as external circumstances changed and as remedial measures were brought forward for examination." Andrews, *The Colonial Period of American History*, IV, 326–27.

6. Benjamin Franklin, representative in London of his home colony of Pennsylvania and a little later of Massachusetts as well, remarked that the M.P.'s had to be bribed "to vote according to their consciences," and a modern writer, Lewis Namier, quaintly defends the House of that time because "even so, it [the rotton borough system] was a mark of English freedom and independence, for no one bribes where he can bully." *England in the Age of the American Revolution*, pp. 4–5.

7. Lexicographers seem uncertain whether the word come into English through the French *mélasse*, the Portuguese *melaço*, or the Italian *melassa*, all of which mean the same thing, but in any event it traces eventually back to the late Latin *mellaceum*, a syrup made from honey (*mel*).

8. "I know not why we should blush to confess that molasses was an essential ingredient in American independence." Adams, *Works*, X, 345.

9. Gin at this time was almost unknown in the colonies, though exceedingly popular, to the point of scandal, at Home; whiskey was rare; French brandy was only for the rich. Rum therefore came to be a generic name for any spirits, as it still is: thus, Demon Rum, Rum Row, etc.

10. "No historic fact can be more clearly shown than that the contest, the threshold of which we have now reached, was really not one between England and America, but a dispute which went on both in England and America, in each land between parties not far from equal in strength. In America the strife was bloody but not prolonged; in England it was bloodless, but very gradual, the closing scenes of the struggle not being unfolded until our own time." Hosmer, *The Life of Thomas Hutchinson*, p. 71.

11. Becker, *The Eve of the Revolution*, p. 15.

12. They did not in fact do so until the year 1847. This was due in part to an unforseeable increase in the rate of population growth in Great Britain, and in part to a complete falling-off, during the long years of the Revolution, of emigration to America.

13. The towns of Barre, Massachusetts, and Barre, Vermont, were both named after him. Neither town uses the acute accent, but each pronounces the word as though it were spelled "Barry," and the citizens of each are piqued when ignorant outsiders pronounce it as "Bar." The city of Wilkes-Barre, Pennsylvania, named after Colonel Barré and John Wilkes, another eighteenth-century "liberty" figure, is often pronounced as though it were Wilkes-Berry.

14. These outlandish, scarecrowish figures were, of course, the original "guys." The word is invariably pejorative among Englishmen, who are startled when they hear Americans refer to "nice guys" or "good guys."

15. Professor Labaree, in his *Royal Government in*

America, Chapter VIII, makes the point that only four times in the thirteen pre-Revolutionary colonies was a royal governor's pay held up, even temporarily. But the *threat* was always there, as the men at Home knew. Those governors were granted a great deal of grandeur—salutes, fanfares, bodyguards, glittering epaulettes, their wives called "lady," and all the rest—but they had not gone out into the howling wilderness (as most of them regarded it) simply for that. If they were to spend three or four years among yokels, thousands of miles away from Almack's, White's, Boodle's, the rotunda at Ranelagh—in short, away from civilization—then they expected at least to be able to retire on what they made; so that when a legislature growled in its fiscal throat they heeded, and heeded well. It was one of the reforms that Grenville most ardently sought—to make the governors financially independent of the elected colonial bodies.

16. "Before the outbreak of the great controversy between the colonies and the British government, no other man in America had, to so high a degree as Hutchinson, the confidence both of the British government on the one hand, and of his own countrymen on the other. Had his advice been taken in that controversy by either of the two parties who had so greatly confided in him, the war of the Revolution would have been averted." Tyler, *The Literary History of the American Revolution*, II, 396–97.

17. "The arrogance and blind indifference with which the sentiments and petitions of the colonists were treated during the enactment of this fatal measure [the Stamp Act] place the responsibility for the American Revolution squarely on the shoulders of the British government." Howard, *Preliminaries of the Revolution, 1763–1775*, p. 136.

18. Conway, Massachusetts, and Conway, New Hampshire, were to be named after *him*.

19. Morgan, *The Stamp Act Crisis: Prologue to Revolution*, p. 91.

20. Thomas Paine's masterpiece, *Common Sense*, was first published anonymously, and there were thousands at that time who assumed that Samuel Adams was the author. "Like cannon balls which sink the ship, and then are lost in the sea, so the bolts of Samuel Adams, after riddling British authority in America, must be sought by diving beneath the oblivion that has rolled over them." (Hosmer, *Samuel Adams*, p. 360.) Tyler Says (*The Literary History of the American Revolution*, II, 2): "Samuel Adams was, indeed, a man of letters, but he was so only because he was above all things a man of affairs. Of literary art, in certain forms, he was no mean master: of literary art for art's sake, he was entirely regardless. He was perhaps the most voluminous political writer of his time in New England; but everything that he wrote was meant for a definite practical purpose, and nothing that he wrote seemed to have an interest for him aside from that purpose."

21. Except that, at just this time, there was a small section of a Scottish regiment stationed in the old barracks at Third and Green streets, Philadelphia.

22. Approximately the present Washington and Essex streets.

23. Trampled and muddied, some almost past recognition, these were laboriously retrieved next morning and assembled. The manuscript is at present in the custody of the Division of Archives, Department of the Massachusetts Secretary of State, State House, Boston.

24. Letter to Richard Jackson,

25. "Disallow" or "negative" were the verbs usually used for what today we would call "veto." It was one of the complaints of the colonies that King George still claimed this

right. Not since the days of Queen Anne, half a century earlier, had an English monarch ventured to "disallow" an act of Parliament; but the acts of the colonial legislatures, previously subject to a veto on the part of the royal governor, were fair game.

26. Thus, so careful an historian as Bancroft unequivocally states (*History of the United States*, V, 248) that George III was "crazed" when he assented to the Stamp Act, March 22, 1765. The idea was revived recently by Guttmacher (*see* Bibliography), an American psychiatrist who had studied the medical records (such as those are) and read Grenville's diary; but it would seem to have been triumphantly refuted by Knollenberg (*Origin of the American Revolution, 1759–1766*, pp. 275–81), who after extensive research has been unable to find a shred of evidence to indicate that anybody in 1765 suspected the presence of even a touch of insanity in George III.

27. Miller, *Origins of the American Revolution*, p. 154.

28. Rowland, *The Life of George Mason*, I, 382.

29. There was a tendency at this time among the American Whigs to glorify King George at the expense of Parliament and the cabinet. He was made out to be an innocent tool in their hands. Virtually every resolution started with a fervent protest of loyalty to the King, and the words "Parliamentary" and "ministerial" often were used as synonyms for "sinister" or even "villainous." This rather startled the English Whigs, who strove to do the very opposite—that is, lessen the power and glory of the King, heightening that of the ministers and of Parliament.

30. "In view of the later revolutionary movement, it is not too much to say that the Stamp Act derived its chief importance from the fact that it lifted the controversy from the profit-and-loss considerations of the northern colonists and

furnished a common ground on which the planting provinces might join with the commercial provinces in protest. The eighteenth-century Anglo-Saxon liked nothing better than the expansive phrases of the natural rights theory; and the Stamp Act readily lent itself to protests against 'taxation without representation' and 'trial by jury'." Schlesinger, *The Colonial Merchants and the American Revolution*, pp. 65–66.

31. Beer, *British Colonial Policy*, p. 301; McClellan, *Smuggling in the American Colonies at the Outbreak of the Revolution, passim.*

32. Nevertheless, as war neared the plans multiplied on both sides of the Atlantic, and after hostilities had broken out there were more of them than ever. The best discussion of this is contained in R. G. Adams, *Political Ideas of the American Revolution* (see Bibliography).

33. Bond, *The Colonial Agent as a Popular Representative*, p. 372; Tanner, *Colonial Agents in England during the Eighteenth Century*, p. 901.

34. "Moreover, just at this moment, when the colonists were tending more and more toward a separation from the mother country as a result of their long independent growth, when their newly-attained freedom from the dangers of French attack made such a divergence, for the first time, possible, and when certain specific encroachments on the part of the English government made it for their interest to stand on their own bottom, they were hardly in a position to accept any innovation which would offer the least menace to their liberties. Hence the efforts of the Episcopalians to push their plan at this time was at least one of the causes tending to accentuate that growing alienation between Great Britain and her colonial subjects beyond the seas which prepared the ground for the Revolution soon to follow." Cross, *The Anglican Episcopate and the American Colonies*, p. 157.

35. The first Church of England bishopric to be established outside of the British Isles was the see of Nova Scotia, in 1787. It was still the only one at the end of the eighteenth century, by which time Spain had established seven archbishoprics and forty-one bishoprics in the New World. The second Church of England bishopric outside of the British Isles was that of Calcutta, set up in 1814. Sweet, *Religion in Colonial America*, p. 66.

36. Hinkhouse, *The Preliminaries of the American Revolution as Seen in the English Press*, p. 127.

37. They had bought the house from John Tathouse, for £600. It was never occupied, and later it was burned down. Manross, *A History of the American Episcopal Church*, Chap. VIII.

38. Born in Trappe, Pennsylvania, he had gone to Germany to study for the church—the Lutheran church. He found when he returned to America and tried to take up a parish in Virginia that he would not be permitted to practice as a preacher unless he was an Anglican divine—not in Virginia, that is. Undaunted, he went to England for a year, where he studied further, and where he took holy orders, returning to America as a sort of Anglo-Lutheran. Anyway he got a parish in Woodstock, Virginia, where he was also colonel of the local militia, and it was from that pulpit, on a Sunday morning in January of 1776, that he preached his celebrated sermon from the third chapter of Ecclesiastes: "To every thing there is a season, and a time for every purpose under the heaven: A time to be born, and a time to die; a time to plant, and a time to pluck up that which is planted . . . a time . . . a time . . ." When he was finished he added, on his own, that there was also a time to pray and a time to fight, and this, he considered, was a time to fight. So he peeled off his clerical robe, and lo and behold the parson was wearing his colonel's

uniform beneath it. He marched outside and took over his assembled troops, and they went off to join the Continental Army. Muhlenberg, a brigadier most of the time, and a good one, was no summer soldier. He stuck it out through all those eight bitter years. Then he went back to his pulpit.

39. Tyler, *The Literary History of the American Revolution*, I, 135.

40. Manross, *A History of the American Episcopal Church*, Chap. VIII.

41. "If Americans could swallow the absurdity that there was a real difference between internal and external taxes, this proved, at least to Townshend's satisfaction, that they were a singularly doltish people who might easily be duped into paying taxes provided they were not called taxes. Townshend's attitude toward the colonists was not altogether dissimilar to that of a shell-game operator toward bumpkins at a country fair. Of course, they would fight if they were held up—the Stamp Act proved that—but Townshend, like a good bunco artist, preferred to trick them out of their money." Miller, *Origins of the American Revolution*, p. 251.

42. "Had it not been for the unfortunate personalities of Robinson, Paxton, and Hulton (three customs officials at Boston) there might have been no Revolution." Dickerson, *The Navigation Acts and the American Revolution*, p. 210. This is putting it too strong; but beyond doubt the new men did not bestir themselves to be pleasant. Also, there were many more of them than before. They seemed to be everywhere. In the years 1767–69, in Philadelphia, for example, the customshouse force was *trebled*.

43. In fact, Hillsborough did not order the troops sent because of the *Liberty* riot, though that would have been sufficient cause for him; but these two were firmly linked in the popular imagination. The order had been sent several

weeks before the secretary of state for the colonies heard of the riot.

Two regiments may seem, to modern readers, an unwieldly force to keep order in a town of 15,000—perhaps double that if the outlying towns are considered; but on this occasion it was to prove too small. A British Army regiment at that time theoretically was made up of 35 officers, 32 non-coms, and 390 rank-and-file, the last including bakers, musicians, and other non-combatants; but very few of them were up to authorized strength, and they were plagued with sickness and desertion. Lieutenant Colonel William Dalrymple, the commanding officer except when Gage himself happened to be present, might have had 600 effectives. Dalrymple was the senior lieutenant colonel. There would be no colonel. Colonels were not field officers but proprietors, capitalists. They were investors, for colonelcies were bought and sold. A colonel *could be* a military man, but that would constitute a coincidence. He could also be a baby.

As to the advisability of sending any troops at all, an American authority:

"However justifiable the action may have appeared from an administrative point of view, the British government made a bad tactical error in sending soldiers to Boston. The statesmanlike policy of maintaining a standing army to protect the empire from foreign enemies had degenerated into an employment of the troops as a military police to enforce hated laws on the people themselves." Schlesinger, *The Colonial Merchants and the American Revolution*, p. 104.

And a British authority:

"Without entering into any discussion as to the right or expediency of resorting to coercion at Boston, it is certain that, if troops were to be employed at all, they should have been employed in sufficient strength and with sufficient powers. Two weak battalions, together barely numbering eight hundred men, were not an adequate force; and even though these were augmented in January, 1769, by the arrival of the Sixty-fourth and Sixty-fifth, yet they still remained powerless to act until called in by the civil power. To invoke their aid was more than any magistrate's life was worth; yet the Government in England, though perfectly aware of the fact, gave no instruction to the General to proclaim martial law. The result was that the troops were laid absolutely at the mercy of the mob of Boston." Fortescue, *History of the British Army,* III, 35.

44. Today we would describe this as a boycott. The word did not exist then. It came into being in the fall of 1880 when Captain Charles Cunningham Boycott, land agent for the estates of the Earl of Erne, County Mayo, Ireland, tried to raise the rents, and the Irish Land League arranged that his servants left him and that nobody would talk to him or deal with him in any way. That is, he was boycotted. The word caught on, proving that there had existed a need for it. It was taken up by the Dutch, Germans, French, Russians, and of course Americans.

45. "From 1768 to 1772 almost open warfare existed between the agents of the Commissioners and the trading fraternity of New England and some of the other major ports." Dickerson, *The Navigation Acts and the American Revolution,* p. 210.

46. Now Portland, Maine. Maine at that time was a part of Massachusetts.

47. The Boston Sons of Liberty, carefully coached in the value of names, always referred to this scuffle as "the attempted assassination of Mr. Otis." From the first, Otis had been a highly emotional person, given to dark doubts, wild flights of fancy, black rages; but after the business at the British Coffee House he was given to spells of utter irresponsibility, which became more frequent until it was thought best

to send him out into the country, to the home of a friend in Andover. From there, in lucid intervals, he witnessed the Revolution, the coming of independence. There, in a raging thunderstorm, Friday afternoon, May 23, 1783, he was standing in an open doorway, telling a story, when a bolt of lightning came down the chimney and split open the door at his side. Otis fell dead on the spot. There was no mark on his body, nor was there any expression of pain on his face, and of the seven or eight other persons nearby none was hurt. Otis had become extremely fat, and that might account for it. In any event, it was fitting finish for so tempestuous a life. Tudor, *The Life of James Otis, of Massachusetts*, p. 485.

48. In a letter to General Charles Lee in New York, from Philadelphia, February 11, 1776. There is a photostatic copy in the Franklin Library at Yale. The original is in the hands of a private collector in California. Franklin—and others who favored the long bow, for he was not alone—pointed out that there was plenty of wood and gut in America but precious little metal; that a bowman could march faster than a musketeer, his weapon being lighter; that the obstruction of smoke would be obviated; that arrows could be recovered from the field and used again; that four arrows could be shot in the time it took to shoot and reload a musket; and that a flight of arrows coming toward a man would scare him, while he could not see a musket ball.

49. Soldiers would work for considerably less than the going rates of labor, which did not endear them to the natives. Kidder, *History of the Boston Massacre*. "The hostility of the Boston workmen to the Red Coat on the eve of the Revolution stemmed in part at least from resentment of the interloper, for the men of the regular army were allowed to accept private employment when they did not have military assignments." Adams, *Government and Labor*, p. 190.

50. The late John F. Kennedy (*Profiles in Courage*, p.

235) called this "an act of courage which preceded the founding of this nation, and which set a standard for all to follow."

51. The date was celebrated for years in Boston, in the Old South Church, with the famous Fifth of March Orations, each delivered to a packed house by some noted patriot. Six years later the commander of the siege of Boston, a tall aloof Virginian named Washington, was to pick March 5 as the date for one last grand assault against the city (an assault that never was made, for it was not needed) because he knew that the eastern Massachusetts men, who made up so much of his force, would fight all the better on such a day. The Fifth of March Orations were discontinued in 1783— or rather, they were switched to July fourth.

52. R. G. Adams, *New Light on the Boston Massacre*, p. 287.

53. He was to become one of the signers of the Declaration of Independence.

54. Hinkhouse, *The Preliminaries of the American Revolution as Seen in the English Press*, p. 155.

55. He was "a commander who among the old sea-dogs of England seems to have been marked by characteristics especially canine." Hosmer, *Samuel Adams*, p. 191.

56. Dudingston recovered, and was promoted to captain. Bartlett, *A History of the Destruction of His Britannic Majesty's Schooner* Gaspee, *passim*. This is the best account of the incident; but it is a hard book to find (*see* Bibliography).

57. This is the opinion of Franklin's best biographer, Carl van Doren. *Benjamin Franklin*, pp. 440–78.

58. "It [the tea act] was so far from being tyrannous and cruel that it was pitiable; pitiable for a proud nation to be reduced to such straits for controlling its colonies." Fisher, *The Struggle for American Independence*, I, 167.

59. Only three ships were to be involved in the Boston

Tea Party, as told in Chapter 1, but a fourth, which was late, was wrecked off Cape Cod. A large part of the tea from this vessel was salvaged by the military and locked in Castle William for safekeeping.

60. Who was to become a general in the Continental Army and after the Revolution the nation's first Secretary of War.

61. If the word has a modern sound, this is only because it lately came back into underworld fashion, as English words have a habit of doing. Actually it is old. Shakespeare uses it (in *As You Like It*), and Peele did so before him. It was originally a shortening of the Italian *capriole*, a frisky dance step, but it very early took on the related meaning of some manner of suspected and fast trick—what a later generation was to call "monkeyshines." It has no connection with the flower buds that are used for pickling: that "caper" is from *Capparis spinosa*, a bush similar to the common bramble, from which those buds are picked. The word also at one time, as a verb, meant to steal at sea, to piratize; but this meaning, originally Dutch, has died.

62. Eventually it was sold at public auction for the benefit of the state of South Carolina. The Revolution was in progress by that time, and the tea was seized just like any other enemy property.

63. He was offered a baronetcy but said no because he did not think that he had a large enough fortune to keep up the dignity. He was retained as a sort of distinguished but unofficial ministerial advisor on American affairs, though his advice does not seem to have been taken very often. He never did return to America. He never dared to. He died and was buried in England, far from the land that he loved.

BIBLIOGRAPHY

ADAMS, CHARLES FRANCIS, see ADAMS, JOHN.

ADAMS, JOHN, *The Works of John Adams, Second President of the United States*, edited by Charles Francis Adams. 10 vols. Boston: Little, Brown and Company, 1850–56.

ADAMS, RANDOLPH G. *New Light on the Boston Massacre.* (Proceedings of the American Antiquarian Society, new series, No. 47, pp. 259–354.) Worcester, Mass., 1938.

——*Political Ideas of the American Revolution: Britannic-American Contributions to the Problem of Imperial Organization, 1765 to 1775.* 3rd edition. New York: Barnes & Noble, Inc., 1958.

ANDERSON, GEORGE P. *Ebenezer Mackintosh: Stamp Act Rioter and Patriot.* Publications of the Colonial Society of Massachusetts, Vol. XXVI.

ANDREWS, CHARLES M. *The Colonial Background of the American Revolution.* New Haven: Yale University Press, 1942.
——*The Colonial Period of American History,* 4 vols. New Haven: Yale University Press, 1938.

BALDWIN, ALICE M. *The New England Clergy and the Revolution.* Durham, N.C.: Duke University Press, 1928.

BANCROFT, GEORGE. *History of the United States,* 6 vols. Boston: Little, Brown and Company, 1876.

BARTLETT, JOHN RUSSEL. *A History of the Destruction of His Britannic Majesty's Schooner* Gaspee. Providence, R.I.: A. Crawford Greene, 1861.

BECKER, CARL. *The Eve of the Revolution: A Chronicle of the Breach with England.* New Haven: Yale University Press, 1918.

BEER, GEORGE LOUIS. *British Colonial Policy, 1754-1765.* New York: The Macmillan Company, 1907.
———*The Commercial Policy of England toward the American Colonies.* New York: Columbia University Press, 1893.

BISHOP, CORTLANDT F. *History of Elections in the American Colonies.* New York: Columbia University Press, 1893.

BOND, BEVERLY W., Jr. "The Colonial Agent as a Popular Representative," *Political Science Quarterly*, XXXV, 372-92.

BOORSTIN, DANIEL J. *The Americans: The Colonial Experience.* New York: Random House, Inc., 1958.

BOTTA, CHARLES. *History of the War of the Independence of the United States of America,* 8th ed., 2 vols. Translated from the Italian by George Alexander Otis. New Haven: T. Brainard, 1840.

BOWEN, CATHERINE DRINKER. *John Adams and the American Revolution.* Boston: Little, Brown and Company, 1950.

BRENNAN, ELLEN ELIZABETH. "James Otis: Recreant and Patriot," *New England Quarterly*, Vol. XII, 691-725.

BROWN, ALEXANDER (ed.). *The Genesis of the United States: Being a Series of Historical Manuscripts,* 2 vols. Boston: Houghton, Mifflin and Company, 1891.

BROWN, MRS. REBECCA. *Stories about General Warren in Relations to the Fifth of March Massacre and the Battle of Bunker Hill.* Boston: James Loring, 1825.

BROWN, WELDON A. *Empire or Independence: A Study in the Failure of Reconciliation, 1774–1783.* Baton Rouge: Louisiana State University Press, 1941.

BUCK, PHILIP W. *The Politics of Mercantilism.* New York: Henry Holt and Company, 1942.

CARY, JOHN. *Joseph Warren: Physician, Politician, Patriot.* Urbana: University of Illinois Press, 1961.

CHANNING, EDWARD. *A History of the United States,* 6 vols. New York: The Macmillan Company, 1905–25.

CLARK, DORA MAE. *British Opinion and the American Revolution.* New Haven: Yale University Press, 1930.

CLARKE, MARY PATTERSON. *Parliamentary Privilege in the American Colonies.* New Haven: Yale University Press, 1943.
——"The Board of Trade at Work," *American Historical Review,* XVII, 17–43.

CROSS, A. L. *The Anglican Episcopate and the American Colonies.* New York: Longmans, Green, and Co., 1902.

CURTIS, EDWARD ELY. *The Organization of the British Army in the Revolution.* New Haven: Yale University Press, 1926.

DAVIDSON, ELIZABETH H. *The Establishment of the English Church in Continental American Colonies.* Durham, N.C.: Duke University Press, 1936.

DAVIDSON, PHILIP. *Propaganda and the American Revolution, 1763–1783.* Chapel Hill: University of North Carolina Press, 1941.

DICKERSON, OLIVER MORTON. *American Colonial Government, 1696–1765: A Study of the British Board of Trade in its Relation to the American Colonies, Political, Industrial, Administrative.* Cleveland, Ohio: The Arthur H. Clark Company, 1912.
——*The Navigation Acts and the American Revolution.* Philadelphia: University of Pennsylvania Press, 1951.

DRAKE, FRANCIS S. (ed.). *Tea Leaves: Being a Collection of Letters and Documents Relating to the Shipment of Tea to the American Colonies in the Year 1773 by the East India Tea Company.* Boston: A. O. Crane, 1884.

ELDON, CARL WILLIAM. *England's Subsidy Policy towards the Continental Colonies during the Seven Years War.* Philadelphia: University of Pennsylvania Press, 1938.

FALKNER, LEONARD. *Forge of Liberty.* New York: E. P. Dutton and Co., Inc., 1959.

FARRAND, MAX. "The Taxation of Tea, 1767–1773," *American Historical Review*, III, 266–69.

FISHER, SYDNEY GEORGE. *The Struggle for American Independence*, 2 vols. Philadelphia, J. B. Lippincott Company, 1909.

FISKE, JOHN. *The American Revolution*, 2 vols. Boston: Houghton, Mifflin and Company, 1897.

FORTESCUE, SIR JOHN WILLIAM. *History of the British Army*, 10 vols. New York: The Macmillan Company, 1899–1920.

FROTHINGHAM, RICHARD. "The Boston Tea-Party," *Proceedings of the Massachusetts Historical Society*, XIII, 154–62. Boston, 1865.
——*The Life and Times of Joseph Warren.* Boston: Little, Brown, and Company, 1865.

——*The Rise of the Republic of the United States*, 10th ed. Boston: Little, Brown, and Company, 1910.

GIPSON, LAWRENCE HENRY. *Aspects of the Beginning of the American Revolution in Massachusetts Bay, 1760–1762.* (Proceedings of the American Antiquarian Society, Vol. LXII, new series.)
——*The Coming of the American Revolution, 1763–1775.* New York: Harper & Brothers, 1954.
——*Jared Ingersoll: a Study of American Loyalism in Relation to British Colonial Government.* New Haven: Yale University Press, 1920.

GORDON, WILLIAM. *The History of the Rise, Progress, and Establishment of the Independence of the United States of America,* 4 vols. London: Printed for the author, 1788.

GRANGER, BRUCE INGRAM. *Political Satire in the American Revolution, 1763–1783.* Ithaca, N.Y.: Cornell University Press, 1960.

GUTTMACHER, MANFRED S. *America's Last King: An Interpretation of the Madness of George III.* New York: Charles Scribner's Sons, 1941.

GRANT, WILLIAM L. "Canada versus Guadeloupe, an Episode of Seven Years' War." *American Historical Review,* XVII, 735–43.

GREEN, SAMUEL A. *The Boston Massacre, March 5, 1770.* (Proceedings of the American Antiquarian Society, new series, Vol. XIV, pp. 40–53.) Worcester, Mass., 1902.

HALL, HUBERT. "Chatham's Colonial Policy," *American Historical Review,* V, 659–75.

HARLOW, RALPH VOLNEY. *Samuel Adams, Promoter of the American Revolution: A Study in Psychology and Politics.* New York: Henry Holt and Company, 1923.

HAWKES, JAMES A. *Retrospect of the Boston Tea-Party.* New York: S. S. Bliss, 1834.

HECKSCHER, ELI F. *Mercantilism.* Translated from the Swedish by Mendel Shapiro. London: G. Allen & Unwin, Ltd., 1935.

HICKHOUSE, FRED JUNKIN. *The Preliminaries of the American Revolution as Seen in the English Press.* New York: Columbia University Press, 1926.

HORROCKS, JOHN WESLEY. *A Short History of Mercantilism.* London: Methuen & Co., 1925.

HOSMER, JAMES K. *Samuel Adams.* Boston: Houghton, Mifflin and Company, 1885.
——*The Life of Thomas Hutchinson, Royal Governor of the Province of Massachusetts Bay.* Boston: Houghton, Mifflin and Company, 1896.

HOWARD, GEORGE ELLIOTT. *Preliminaries of the Revolution, 1763–1775.* New York: Harper & Brothers, 1905.

HUTCHINSON, PETER ORLANDO (ed.). *The Diary and Letters of His Excellency Thomas Hutchinson, Esq.,* 2 vols. Boston: Houghton, Mifflin and Company, 1886.

HUTCHINSON, THOMAS. *History of the Province of Massachusetts Bay.* Vol. III (from 1750 until June, 1774). London, 1828.

JAMESON, J. FRANKLIN. *The American Revolution Considered as a Social Movement.* Boston: Beacon Press, 1961.

JONES, THOMAS. *History of New York during the Revolutionary War,* 2 vols. New York: New-York Historical Society, 1879.

KIDDER, FREDERIC. *History of the Boston Massacre, March 5, 1770.* Albany, N.Y.: Joel Munsell, 1870.

KNOLLENBERG, BERNHARD. *Origin of the American Revolution, 1759–1766.* New York: The Macmillan Company, 1960.
———*Did Sam Adams Provoke the Boston Tea Party and the Clash at Lexington?* (American Antiquarian Society Proceedings, new series, LXX, 493–503.)

LABAREE, BENJAMIN W. *The Boston Tea Party.* New York: Oxford University Press, 1964.

LABAREE, LEONARD W. *Royal Government in America: A Study of the British Colonial System before 1783.* New York: Frederick Ungar Publishing Company, 1958.

LAPRADE, W. T. "The Stamp Act in British Politics," *American Historical Review,* Vol. XXXV, no. 4, pp. 735–57.

LECKY, W. E. H. *History of England in the Eighteenth Century,* 8 vols. London: Longmans, Green & Co., 1878–90.

LONG, J. C. *Mr. Pitt and America's Birthright.* New York: Frederick A. Stokes, Inc., 1940.

LONN, ELLA. *The Colonial Agents of the Southern Colonies.* Chapel Hill: University of North Carolina Press, 1945.

MANROSS, WILLIAM WILSON. *A History of the American Episcopal Church*. New York and Milwaukee: Morehouse Publishing Co., 1935.

McCLENNAN, WILLIAM S. *Smuggling in the American Colonies at the Outbreak of the Revolution, with Special Reference to the West Indies Trade*. New York: Moffat, Yard and Company, 1912.

MILLER, JOHN C. *Origins of the American Revolution*. Boston: Little, Brown and Company, 1948.
———. *Sam Adams, Pioneer in Propaganda*. Boston: Little, Brown and Company, 1936.

MILLER, PERRY. *The New England Mind*. New York: The Macmillan Company, 1939.

MORGAN, EDMUND S. "Thomas Hutchinson and the Stamp Act," *New England Quarterly* (December, 1948), 459–92.
———(ed.). *Prologue to Revolution: Sources and Documents on the Stamp Act Crisis, 1764–1766*. Chapel Hill: University of North Carolina Press, 1959.
———*The Birth of the Republic, 1763–89*. Chicago: University of Chicago Press, 1956.
———and MORGAN, HELEN M. *The Stamp Act Crisis: Prologue to Revolution*. Chapel Hill: University of North Carolina Press, 1953.

MORRIS, RICHARD B. *Government and Labor in Early America*. New York: Columbia University Press, 1946.
———(ed.). *The Era of the American Revolution*. New York: Columbia University Press, 1939.

MORSE, JOHN T. *John Adams*. Boston: Houghton, Mifflin and Company, 1899.

NAMIER, LEWIS. *Charles Townshend; His Character and Career*. Cambridge: Cambridge University Press, 1959.
———*England in the Age of the American Revolution*. London: Macmillan and Company, Ltd., 1930.

NORTH, LORD. "Lord North, the Prime Minister: A Personal Memoir," *North American Review*, CLXXVI, 778–91, and CLXXVII, 260–77.

OLIVER, PETER. *Origin and Progress of the American Rebellion: A Tory View*, edited by Douglass Adair and John A. Schutz. San Marino, Calif.: The Huntington Library, 1961.

OTIS, GEORGE ALEXANDER, see BOTTA, CHARLES.

PARES, RICHARD. *King George III and the Politicians*. New York: Clarendon Press (Oxford), 1953.
——*Merchants and Planters*. Cambridge: Cambridge University Press, 1960.
——*Yankees and Creoles: The Trade between North America and the West Indies before the American Revolution*. Cambridge: Harvard University Press, 1952.

PEABODY, ANDREW PRESTON. "Boston Mobs before the Revolution," *Atlantic Monthly*, LXII, (September 1888), 321–33.

RAGATZ, LOWELL, JOSEPH. *The Fall of the Planter Class in the British Caribbean, 1763–1833*. New York: The Century Company, 1928.

RITCHESON, CHARLES R. *British Politics and the American Revolution*. Norman, Okla.: University of Oklahoma Press, 1954.

ROSSITER, CLINTON. *Seedtime of the Republic: The Origin of the American Tradition of Political Liberty*. New York: Harcourt, Brace and Co., 1953.

ROWLAND, KATE MASON. *The Life of George Mason, 1725–1792*, 2 vols. New York: G. P. Putnam's Sons, 1892.

SCHLESINGER, ARTHUR MEIER. *Prelude to Independence: The Newspaper War on Britain*. New York: Alfred A. Knopf, Inc., 1958.
——"The American Revolution Reconsidered," *Political Science Quarterly*, XXXIV, 61–78.
——*The Colonial Merchants and the American Revolution*. New York: The Facsimile Library, 1939.

SCHMOLLER, GUSTAV. *The Mercantile System and Its Historical Significance.* New York: Macmillan and Company, 1896.

SCHUTZ, JOHN A., see OLIVER, PETER.

SHAPIRO, MENDEL, see HECKSCHER, ELI F.

SUTHERLAND, STELLA H. *Population Distribution in Colonial America.* New York: Columbia University Press, 1956.

SWEET, WILLIAM WARREN. *Religion in Colonial America.* New York: Charles Scribner's Sons, 1942.

TANNER, EDWIN P. "Colonial Agents in England during the Eighteenth Century." *Political Science Quarterly*, XVI, 901. 901.

TAWNEY, R. H. *Religion and the Rise of Capitalism.* Harmondsworth, England: Penguin Books, Ltd., 1938.

TAYLOR, EMERSON. *Paul Revere.* New York: Edward Valentine and Dodd, Mead & Company, 1930.

THATCHER, B. B. *Traits of the Tea Party: Being a Memoir of George R. T. Hewes, One of the Last of its Survivors; With a History of that Transaction.* New York: Harper & Brothers, 1835.

THORNTON, JOHN WINGATE. *The Pulpit of the American Revolution.* Boston: Gould and Lincoln, 1860.

TIFFANY, C. C. *A History of the Protestant Episcopal Church in the United States of America.* New York: Charles Scribner's Sons, 1899.

TREVELYAN, SIR GEORGE OTTO. *The American Revolution*, 4 vols. New York: Longmans, Green, and Co., 1905.

TUTOR, WILLIAM. *The Life of James Otis, of Massachusetts.* Boston: Wells and Lilly, 1823.

TURBERVILLE, A. S. *English Men and Manners in the 18th Century.* New York: Oxford University Press, 1957.

TYLER, MOSES COIT. *Patrick Henry*. Boston: Houghton, Mifflin and Company, 1898.

——*The Literary History of the American Revolution*, 2 vols. New York: G. P. Putnam's Sons, 1897.

VAN DOREN, CARL. *Benjamin Franklin*. New York: The Viking Press, 1938.

VAN TYNE, CLAUDE H. *The Causes of the War of Independence*. Boston: Houghton Mifflin Company, 1922.

WALSH, CORREA MOYLAN. *The Political Science of John Adams*. New York: G. P. Putnam's Sons, 1915.

WELLS, WILLIAM VINCENT. *The Life and Public Services of Samuel Adams*. Boston: Little, Brown, and Company, 1865.

INDEX

INDEX

www.ingramcontent.com/pod-product-compliance
Lightning Source LLC
Chambersburg PA
CBHW021228090426
42740CB00006B/434